Katie-Jane Wright

Songs of the Stones

Crystals to Connect with
the Ancestors and the Earth

WATKINS

Songs of the Stones
Katie-Jane Wright

First published in the UK and USA in 2025 by
Watkins, an imprint of Watkins Media Limited
Unit 11, Shepperton House, 83–89 Shepperton Road
London N1 3DF

enquiries@watkinspublishing.com

Commissioning Editor: Sophie Blackman
Project Editor: Brittany Willis
Head of Design: Karen Smith
Designer: Alice Claire Coleman
Commissioned Photography: Caitlin Callahan
Production: Uzma Taj

Printed in China

A CIP record for this book is available from the British Library

ISBN: 978-1-78678-948-8 (Paperback)
ISBN: 978-1-78678-949-5 (eBook)

10 9 8 7 6 5 4 3 2 1

www.watkinspublishing.com

The manufacturer's authorised
representative in the EU
for product safety is
eucomply OÜ - Pärnu mnt 139b-14,
11317 Tallinn, Estonia,
hello@eucompliancepartner.
com,www.eucompliancepartner.com

MIX
Paper | Supporting
responsible forestry
FSC® C104723

Connecting with crystalline grids
of light above and below.

This is for my grandmother,
my ancestors and my son.

This book will bring us back to the
power of the Earth and its rituals, helping
us to connect with ourselves. We are a
reflection of the Earth, and all the beauty
of the Earth is within us. With this book,
we will dive deeper into the stories
and messages of the stones, the Earth,
your ancestors and the guardians of the
stones that over-light their energy.

The Moon Gate. I often witness the energies of the universe flow through the limestone giants at this moon gate at Avebury Stones. It felt a fitting gateway for starting our journey together.

Contents

Diamond grid gathering in Sedona, Arizona, working and crystal gridding with the Earth energies and guardians at Oak Creek.

Connecting With the Stones

I invite you to journey with me and the stone keepers through ancient lands.

Through this book you will walk with us and forge a deeper connection to your ancestors. You will ask deeper questions of yourself as the wisdom of the stones envelops you and invites you into new streams of consciousness. I will offer you insight into these, but it is not my place to tell you how to work with these gifts of the Earth.

This book embodies the "Spirit of the Stones". I believe that each stone has an elemental, deva energy. They are part of the force of nature, which connects the whole of nature. Over time this energy builds up and is added to by the people and beings around it, because every energy around a stone leaves its trace. And it is through these traces of energy that we can listen to the stories of the Earth's ancestral protectors. It is my wish to carry the stories of the stones forward with respect and humility.

In many cultures, stories and traditions are being lost because they are not being passed down. As in my ancestral culture, the Khasi people of northeast India, stories are often passed down orally, and there is no written document of their rituals or energies. On this Earth walk I am part of this matriarchal Indian tribe, but I speak about other tribes and cultures I am not part of directly, but I feel their energy sing so strongly through my heart when they speak to me directly. I have had many past lives in some of these cultures and the source of information in the book is the Earth, and her guardians, the council of elders that speak through the pages. The information you will read comes directly from them: a conversation with the ancient Earth council. I also believe that we are all woven as one, and as a collective race we are moving toward unity consciousness, acceptance and love. I approach all my practices with respect, and I hope that you feel this through the book. It was written in and with love and respect for everyone.

I have travelled to many sacred sites across the world to connect with the stones, and I will share these stories in this book. There are giant sarsen stones in the outer circle of Stonehenge that sing loudest when it rains, speaking of the way water enhances and amplifies their energy. In the sacred Corycian Cave in Delphi, high up on Mount Parnassus, where the oracles met to divinate with stone and bone, there's a guard rock and a generous rock being who sits with his gnome and nymph guardians, and he offers insight on the portal to inner Earth there.

Photographs are included to support your connections to the wisdom of the stones, and enhance your own personal journey work with them. With light-encoded words and activations, crystal guidance and rituals, this book will open your eyes and heart to new possibilities and new ways of connection with the Earth and the stones that are her bones, as many of your ancestors have before you.

This book connects with the *Songs of the Stones Oracle* deck, and expands on its messages. When writing the *Songs of the Stones Oracle* deck there was so much information and energy coming that it felt right to expand on them in this book, to support the unfolding of a deeper connection for you. Many of the crystals you will read about in this book are in the oracle deck and add more depth to their story.

Connecting with the vortex energies of
Cathedral Rock, Sedona, Arizona.

My Connection to the Stones

Since I was a child, I have collected dusty rocks that spoke to me. My first stone was something I called "moon rock", which I found in the bottom of my garden. My twelve-year-old self knew that it was not actually from the moon, but this dusty, white, porous pebble, with intricate potholes dancing across the surface, sparked curiosity in me. I held this little, unassuming stone every night under my pillow. I felt it grounded and anchored me into my body, and that was something I really needed. You see, from a very young age, I travelled at night, lucid dreaming and poring over my records with my spirit guides, visiting realms where crystals were as big as houses. Crystal devas, the souls of the stones, spoke to me; they love to dance and sing their songs for all who will listen.

I remember being really respectful even at a young age. I asked the Earth if I could please have this stone for a little while until it was ready to move on, and I listened for the Earth and its guardians to say yes or no. This is something that seems to have been passed on to my son. Wherever we go on our pilgrimages, if he feels really connected to the land, he collects a stone that calls to him. We have bowls of them all around our home and on his altar. And when he shows me his pockets he instantly says, "Don't worry, Mum, I asked the Earth." It's never said no to him yet: the stones love to assist us in all the ways they can.

Since I was young, I have found myself coming home with pockets of stones, and each one tells a story. These stories are of where they came from, the energies of that land and the

Gridding on the land in the Yucatan, working
with the energies of spirit and place.

voices of the ancestral guardians who worked with them and
protected them.

In this book, I wanted to tell these stories. They are from
special stones in the many sacred sites across the world that I
have travelled to, from the red rock of Sedona, to the limestone
caves of the Magdalene in the south of France to the carnelians
of Washington state.

These stones have found me in the most magical and synchronistic ways, along with the musings of the crystal devas, and the spirits of the ancestors that speak through them. I have met many people along the way who adore them as much as me. All of this wisdom fosters a deeper connection and resonance with the Earth through us, and it will spark connections for you, bringing you the stones' remembrances, through their words, which are steeped in Earth energies of love and unity.

I am hugely passionate about keeping these stories alive. I feel that human connection to each other through the heart is what

Working with the energies of the red rock vortexes to anchor and amplify light as a crystalline being.

life is about, and that a chance encounter with a stranger is not chance at all. Every person, stone, plant, animal or insect we encounter we were *meant* to connect with. Everyone has a story to tell and I have always wanted to tell them. At every sacred site or stone circle I meet the most amazing and interesting people who have these stories to tell of how they connect with the stones, and how the stones foster connection through their family and community.

When we connect with the stones, it is just as important to welcome and connect with their ancestral guardians and spirit of the land they came from. When we do this, we gain a rounded picture of the stones' uses and energies through the ages.

Geology is not my area of expertise. I am a translator of the stones' energy. I shy away from the word "channel" as I feel this book holds a co-creation and weaving of many divine energies, and also my own past memories, the memories of my ancestors and my future visions.

Instead of telling you how a crystal or stone works with your energy field, I encourage you to ask of it your own questions, because what I have learnt through my interactions with them is that often they have very specific individual missions of love for you. With this book, I am offering up different perspectives and concepts for you to sit with and consider what they mean to you, and I hope that my stories inspire you, and the colours and images that they conjure help you to connect to their own stories.

This book is intended for people who already have some knowledge of crystals and are looking to take it to the next level, although I feel there is no beginner when it comes to working with crystals, as they are a part of everyone's cosmic heritage.

Calling in the Voice of Your Ancestors

This book is also an opportunity to connect with your ancestors. Their stories make up our own, and so all ancestors' stories in this book are part of your story, and in reading these pages you are bringing yourself closer to them. As we dive through these energies together I invite you to take a breath with me, placing your left hand on your heart, and speak your grandmothers' and grandfathers' names out loud, with love and honour, thanking them for all that they did to pave your way.

The voices of your ancestors make up the songs of the stones, as your ancestors are the ones who tended and cherished the Earth. Since the beginning of time, ancient healers and medicine people have valued the power of stones, sparking legends, mystery and intrigue. And we can still listen and learn from them. Through this book we find that stillness and space to connect with both the voices of the Earth and our ancestors.

This book dives deeper into the crystals, pebbles and shamanic stones of this planet. The word "shamanic" is a spiritual temple that describes a collection of ancestors from different tribes or traditions. My ancestors are shamans, medicine people, and my understanding of this term comes through them. This book is a space to whisper their gifts, as they each have wisdom, personalities and opinions. Each stone wishes to help you connect with the Earth in a deeper way, and each has a message to help you align to its vibration, with new insight and ideas to connect with. This book weaves crystalline activations and crystal grids for meditation, to help deepen the connection to all that you are and can be, but most importantly, to foster that deeper connection to the Earth.

Many new stones are being found across the world, because our human consciousness is ready to receive their gifts and ascension messages. So please, take the parts that resonate at the time of reading, come back and more wisdom will activate and open within you. Take only what feels good and true to you.

One of the most powerful questions you can ask a stone is:

"How do my ancestors know you?"

Your job is to listen and to be open to all of the signs, symbols and insights that drop into your consciousness. They might not awaken and open to you the first time, but be consistent and patient. Build a relationship with them, working with it each day in your daily practices, and they will find you.

> **"The stones show us the footprints of many who have walked before us."**

The stones show us the footprints of many who have walked before us, and to carry their energy is an honour for them. The stones are record keepers, watching and keeping stories for future generations. They are the bones of the Earth, offering us what we need, if only we stay still and listen. They observe, listen and store energy for thousands and millions of years, and then many break down into sand, offering themselves back to the Earth. In one pinch of sand is the memory of hundreds

It is important we offer love to the Earth.
Natural offerings will suffice: things that will
decompose and not harm the environment.

and thousands of living beings. When you are on the beach,
remember that you are sitting on the stories of your ancestors.
I remember one day, when I sitting by the sea feeling all the fine
grains of sand between my feet, turning over a smooth pebble
in my hands and admiring its simple and beautiful aesthetic.
I wondered how I could do more to support this place that I call
home, and I asked the Earth:

"How can I best serve you?"

And the Earth replied –

"Why do you feel I need your service?
All I need is balance.
*Just **be** here with me.*

"I am complete, I flow, expand, release and regulate.
I am whole.
Are you not the same?
Breathe with me as the tide does.

"We are perfection.
Creation is in the eye of the mind and the heart
of the whole.

"Do not busy yourself with what you think you should
be doing, let it flow.

"Be one with the Earth and sky
Be at one with perfection.

*"Just **be**,*
It is all so simple to me."

We do not have to do anything. We just need to be in this space
together and listen.

My Ancestors

My ancestors have a saying:

Mei- Ri- Sawkun

This is an indigenous Khasi concept, meaning:

Mother Earth cradles its children and all else around it.

My ancestors are descendants of the Khasi hill tribe of the Meghalaya hills in northeast India, one of the last two known matrilineal communities in the world. All elder women are referred to as "Mai", which means "mother". They are the head of the family and lead ceremonies. The Khasi people are a forest-dependent community and Khasi healers approach the forest with deep humility and respect. They work with the nature spirits for shelter, firewood, food, medicine and spiritual traditions.

    I was close to my grandmother, who was the first generation of the family to move outside of India. She brought me up, and was always there when I was younger, encouraging me to go barefoot as much as I could outside, and to eat her curries with my hands. I took deep notice of her healing hands, and I remember that whenever I had a tummy ache or pain I asked her to put her hands there and it magically disappeared. I remember her love of flowers and plants, and of being outdoors in nature. She grew tropical

> **"The voices of your ancestors make up the songs of the stones."**

Women of my ancestral Khasi tribe: Katie-Jane's grandmother, great-grandmother, aunties and community.

plants in her conservatory, and my family always just knew to give her plants that were sad or close to the end and she would bring them back to life with ease. She sung to them and spoke to them and they woke from death's door, blooming brighter and fuller. Her gifts were with the plants rather than the stones, but alchemy of plants and minerals go hand in hand.

The Khasi believe that nature is our library. They worked closely with the stones and plants, and many ancient megaliths stand in their sacred groves in the Khasi hills of Meghalaya. These are pockets of ancient forests preserved by the communities for hundreds of years for their ritual and beliefs. "*Meghalaya*" means "abode of clouds"; from the Sanskrit *megha*, meaning "cloud". These forests are some of the richest botanical habitats of Asia, as they receive abundant rainfall and support a rich biodiversity and a vast array of plants that can only be found in that region of the world, as well as being an incredible source for minerals, including limestone and coal.

Who Are Your Ancestors?

We all have a beautiful team of spiritual guides who come to offer us support when we ask for it. These come to us through crystals and stones, because they possess an array of ancestral energy that is stored within their consciousness, through Earth records, from all the hands that have touched, held and worked with them. It is likely that your spirit team is made up of your ancestors. These could be grandparents or great-grandparents you met in life, or much older ancestors you have never met. As we are all connected to the whole, these ancestors could also come from other past lives and lineages you have been woven into. You can call this team of spiritual guides forward at any time, and the words and energies from this book will act as your gateway to them, and anchor their wisdom to you.

My first spirit animal wisdom oracle was a Native American Cherokee man called Big Bear. I have a labradorite carving that looks very much like him.

He seemed to know me very well and referred to me with a chuckle as "Running River" because I was forever

> **"Your ancestral guides can support you in many ways as gatekeepers, protectors and healers."**

on the move. As I was writing this book, he and I held the space around a fire to welcome the animal spirits in to listen to them.

Your ancestral guides can support you in many ways as gatekeepers, protectors and healers. Just ask which of your ancestral guides is with you now, and you may find there are some who appear that you weren't aware of. If you already know who your ancestral spirit guides are, then get ready to meet a whole lot more through these activated words, and I will explain how you can connect with them in the next section.

My grandmother, great grandmother and their community.

The Medicine Hut

At the start of my awakening, over 20 years ago, I created a safe and protected space to meet my own ancestral guides.

I have seen and been very close to the angels since I was a child, so the first space I ever created was in the ninth dimensional angelic planes. It was a light pod that had two doors: one at the front and back to let energy in and out in one direction. I asked two power angels to stand guard as gatekeepers in front of the doors and to only let in beings and energies that were the highest expressions of divine light. It is always important to use discernment too when working with energies and I found this helped protect me from anything untowards.

I would enter my light pod and then call in my guides to talk to, or if I was doing a session with clients I would meet their guides within that space, and in their higher self. All it contained was a table and chairs, and a very pure and brilliant bright, almost blinding white colour. I would meet with multiple beings at once and talk.

I found that when calling ancestral energies in, a different room was needed, and I was asked to create a medicine hut to meet the ancestors in. Perhaps because it was familiar to me and my past experiences, but I have found this hut most useful to connect with the ancestors. My medicine hut is a circular building made of mud and clay with a straw roof. It has two window-like openings and a doorway, and is nestled in a vibrant jungle. When I walk to it barefoot to it the soil smells fresh and alive, and the large tropical leaves are so vibrant and green, full of life-force energy. It exists as a safe pocket of energy on the higher planes of light.

I have found the medicine hut so beneficial for exchanging stories and ideas with my ancestors that I wanted to help you create that pocket of energy too. You can find a guided audio on my website katiejanewright.com called "Visit the Ancestors With the Energy of Flint", that guides you through this journey.

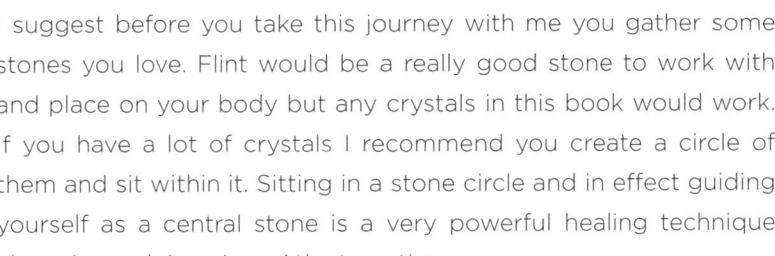

Journey to the Crystal Heart of Gaia

I suggest before you take this journey with me you gather some stones you love. Flint would be a really good stone to work with and place on your body but any crystals in this book would work. If you have a lot of crystals I recommend you create a circle of them and sit within it. Sitting in a stone circle and in effect guiding yourself as a central stone is a very powerful healing technique I have been doing since Atlantean times.

I recommend that you carry out the ritual as you are reading it, opening and closing your eyes when you need to. The words help you create the visuals: you will be in two places at one.

★ Take some time to sit quietly, alone and breathe full, deep breaths into your body to get yourself grounded and centred.
★ It's always good to repeat on every exhale "I am safe in my body" to bring yourself fully into the present moment.
★ Make sure your crystals are close: you are either holding some or sitting in a circle of them.

* Take a moment to connect with each crystal. Stare at them, say hello, touch them, thank them. Feel a collective energy field around them and breathe it into your body as a colour.

* As you slow your body and energy down with your breath, call this energy back into your body from all places and people. Start to listen for your heartbeat.

* Focus on your heartbeat, imagine its sound and the way it feels in your chest and body. Get fully into your heart, sinking into it. And in your heart you begin to see a seed of light form, beautiful and glowing. This seed of light is your love to be planted into the Earth.

* Hold that visual, this seed of love, and when you are ready let it go. As it shoots out of your body and into the Earth, follow its energy down, deeper into the Earth beneath you as it forms a chute of light to ride with.

* Enjoy the ride in, noticing your feelings, the light, your surroundings.

* You begin to feel a magnetizing pull toward Gaia's crystalline heart within the Earth; you feel the Earth's heartbeat ripple through you, and you follow its call.

* You see the crystal heart of the Earth in front of you, pumping love, full of colours and sounds, and you connect your seed of love with it. You connect your heart with it and feel a whoosh of energy move within you. You are connected.

* In this bright place, you are transported to a jungle scene. It forms around you, lush green leaves, vibrant flowers. Feel the smells, the sun, the sounds from birds and the rustle of leaves from the animals hiding.

* You notice a pathway through the jungle and look down at your bare feet on the path, and you follow it into the jungle. As you move through you use all your senses to paint this picture around you. Really feel it in your bones, knowing it exists and that you have painted it into creation.
* In the distance you see a golden glow of a fire, and see smoke rise through the trees. As you approach it a medicine hut comes into view.
* Within there is a fire burning in the centre, and there's talking and laughter and smells of herbs burning, filling the air with clouds of smoke.
* You enter the hut and take the scene in, feeling comfort form the warmth within.
* You see an elder ancestor sitting at the fire. As they invite you to sit with them, the clouds of smoke clear a little and your eyes adjust and you see the eyes of your ancestor smiling at you. You observe their markings or clothes and you may even recognize them. If you feel you wish to, you can ask their name.
* The connection is formed. Now it is up to you to build the connection, to share stories and ask the ancestors questions.

You can sit in the medicine hut for as long as you like as new ancestors come in to gather and talk. You can be the quiet observer or you can ask questions that come to you in the moment. For example: how do I know you? Have you been guiding me for long?

It's good to set the intent to visit the medicine hut before you sleep or in meditation. Journey there and sit with the ancestors for answers.

Crystals to Connect With Your Ancestors

Crystals and stones will help you connect to your ancestors. If you want to connect with someone specific, you could work with ones that this person liked or owned. When a friend of mine needed some healing, she found an old carnelian ring that belonged to her grandmother, and when she wears it she feels her grandmother's energy guiding her closely.

Often my work involves me being called to the bedside of those departing the Earth plane, to ease their crossing and support their family. This role is referred to as being a psychopomp, and this holding open of the gateway of light is done with the angels, and is the greatest honour. This transition of crossing from this life to the other, where the soul lives on, is one of the deepest expressions of love to feel.

When my grandmother was passing she was in hospital, and we were called to her bedside because the nurses felt she was on her way out. She had not drunk for some time and had not opened her eyes or spoken. I arrived at hospital to some emotional cousins sitting at her bedside, telling me that it was the end, encouraging me to say my goodbyes to her. I took my place next to her quiet and still body, and for some reason when I left the house I had brought with me a pile of old black and white photos of her and her family (one of those photos is photographed in this book, see page 19). I put my hand on her heart and just sent as much of my love directly into her heart as I could to warm it up.

Within ten minutes of this something magical happened. As my cousins and I were unknowingly holding space around us, my grandma opened her eyes and looked at me, and she said my name. I carried on holding her heart; I can still feel her warmth and smell the Nivea cream she used religiously. She was the most beautiful person I ever knew, even in death. Within 20 minutes she was sitting up, talking and laughing. The nurses came in and were so surprised. One exclaimed, "Catherine, you're awake!" And my grandma said, "This is my granddaughter Katie-Jane; she has healing hands." We all sat and looked at the photographs and she talked about her family and her home in India. I had this sense of urgency to ask her everything I could about her past, because we don't do this enough while the people we love are here. I realized I had spent all of my life with her and didn't know enough about her life to honour it. I'm crying as I'm writing this: it has brought my love for her flooding back. I guess she noticed my healing hands too.

The story of my grandmother's crossing didn't end there. After a few days she continued to deteriorate so she was moved to a hospice, where a nurse called Venus looked after her. I went to see her and just held her hands and rubbed her feet, which I always did with her. It had been a couple of days and she had not had any water, and we know the end of her Earth walk was soon, so I took my crystal singing bowls and I set them up at her bedside, and with my mother in the room holding her hand I played them, and I sang to her a melody from the heart. At that point she wasn't saying much but she managed to murmur one word after I finished singing: she said, "Beautiful."

I often bring in this ritual when I am called to the bedside of a departing loved one, and it supports their grieving relatives, and connects with their energy after the loved one has gone.

I take my medicine bag of rose and myrrh anointing oils and sprays, fresh roses, as well as a small, heart-shaped carved rose quartz crystal. I ask the relative to hold this the heart of the soul who is close to crossing. We place our hands over this crystal and ask that it attunes with the soul resonance and life-force energy of the person departing. We visualize that pink ray of love travelling from the person's heart space into the crystals. I ask them to pour all of their love and feelings into these crystals. They hold their hands there for as long as they feel they need to, and then thank their relative. They now have a crystal that is carrying the love and energy of that person long after they have left the Earth plane, and it acts as a comfort and connection to them.

Another way of connecting with your ancestors is to work with their birthstone, or you can ask, aloud, "Which crystals would like to help me connect with my ancestor?" and one may eagerly jump forward to you. If you don't know who your ancestral guide is, or aren't getting any intuitive nudges or feelings, that's OK, this is not a test. You could consider using carnelian or amber, or any crystals in this book. You can also try working with this book like a divination deck. Hold it to your heart and ask it to reveal to you the stone you most need to forge a stronger connection to your ancestors. Then visualize your heart chakra opening and surrounding the book in your heart's light. It will be absorbed through the pages. You may then open the book, trusting you will land on the right page, as you would with an oracle card deck. You can also work with the *Songs of the Stones Oracle* deck alongside this book in the same way.

Champagne lemurian quartz charging in the sun.

Collecting Stones From Nature

You do not need to own the most expansive and expensive collection of crystals to awaken and expand further. The Earth is full of richness we can work with. We can ask her, and collect (only) the crystals and stones we need for our journey. We must also gain permission to walk the land to collect crystals and stones where necessary. In this book, we will meet stones that are abundant on the Earth and they hold as much Earth energy as a rare mineral dug from her.

Connecting With the Crystal Energy
Through the Images in This Book

You can also connect with the energies of the stones in this book without owning them yourself. Energy knows no bounds and is fluid and free flowing. All the stones and crystals photographed in this book are my own that I work with regularly, and are very active and alive. To connect with them, all you need to do is ground and centre yourself, gaze at the image of the crystal or stone you wish to connect with and call its energy to flow into your body. It is important to use all your senses to paint the picture of the crystal flowing into you, for example, with stromatolite, imagine it lighting up with brown light as it connects with you and jumps from the page into your heart. There is no judgement or pressure to connect in this way though. Everyone has their own unique way of connecting with energy, but I find painting the picture in your mind as I have outlined creates more of a visual that will strengthen the connection.

The energies of the stones or crystals may wish to jump or flow into different parts of your body. Allow for that, and be curious, following the crystal's flow into your body. Ask yourself how its energy makes you feel. Building a relationship with stones and crystals takes time and dedication, so work at it, examining the connection and its effects on you when you can.

Connecting With the Energies of the Light Language in This Book

You will find light language crystal activations in this book, and you can connect with this light language in a similar way to the images of the crystals. These are formed of golden lines, geometry and coding, present though the illustrations in this book. This light language is not from any alphabet, but is written while I am in a lucid state and connected with crystalline energies and their guardians. These symbols are the coded language of light, and are also present in my *Songs of the Stones Oracle* deck.

We are all made up of light and sound that form sacred geometry, and when we approach this light language, the lightbody, heart and soul recognize it. The light codes in this book support you to open, connect and move energies through your mind, body and spirit. They hold frequencies that activate DNA and stir cellular memories within you. These codes are not ours, but are an expression of energy that flows through and then leaves the lightbody, working with your highest and greatest good. They are created in love with the highest purpose of harmony, peace and deeper connection.

This light-coded frequency offers an opening of
energies within the body, so that more light can flush
into your cells and atoms, to raise your vibration.

The light language comes from the heart, so as you observe
it, it is your heart that must feel it, and there is no need for
your mind to make sense of it. As I am inspired to create it, it is
imbued with energy. It reflects the direction we are all moving
in and expressing from our hearts, with love from our core.

It is very important to remember that the light language speaks to the heart and not the mind. It encourages you to feel, so I would ask that when working with the light language you meditate with the image on page 32. Gently gaze at the light language coding, softening your eyes slightly. Allow it to jump to life in your space and flow through your body and to see where it goes and how it makes your heart feel.

Your Crystal Codex

Stored within your cellular memory is a library of crystal frequencies that you have worked with in your past and that you can call forward to support you. Because your body downloads and remembers all crystalline frequencies you interact with, they weave into the vast fabric of your being and are part of you. It's important to remember this intelligence that is within your lightbody. This memory includes crystals you have connected or worked closely with, and crystals that your ancestors have worked with, as they are part of you.

In the ancient kingdoms of Lemuria and Atlantis, we worked closely with crystals, and this work remains stored within you. In Lemuria, we created crystals through elemental alchemy, while in Atlantis, we worked closely with record-keeper crystals in temples, and these recorded many frequencies coming out of the Earth and grids. Imagine yourself as this quartz record-keeper crystal. Some people like to consciously say, "I download and activate the energy of these ancient crystals within me", but most of the time it is unnecessary because your crystalline nature is always recording this energy and will always remember it. Much of our awareness of crystals was stunted and held on Atlantean timelines, and we are reaching a time where more of these binds are releasing so we can remember the full extent of crystalline technology.

I often witness these crystal libraries in people's lightbodies, and see the ways they understand and move with crystals. For example, red jasper jumps forward to greet me from people's lower chakras. I see the Priestess of Isis in rubies, garnets and obsidian held within lightbodies today. It is interesting to harness and work with these crystals' energies stored in our lightbodies and call them to the surface. We need to work with the crystal to support us in remembering our divine nature, and we also need to harness light with them as amplifiers.

I had a beautiful example of how powerful cellular memory is when I was at the Tucson Gem, Mineral & Fossil Showcase in Phoenix. I had met and connected with some very strong red quartz, which is quartz with a high percentage of iron in it. When I held this piece it dragged me instantly into the Earth. My right hand started to tingle, then a really strong numb feeling came that swept up my whole arm. I had to put the stone down. Later on that day I was talking about that red quartz to a friend and the same numb feeling came instantly to my right arm again, as I had reconnected to its energy, only this time it was nowhere in sight, yet I had made that connection again.

Journey to Open Your Crystal Codex

This is a journey for you to hold the vision of your crystalline DNA and to open your crystalline codex and connect to its memories and experiences.

You will need to place clear quartz on your third eye chakra. You can also intuitively place more crystals on your body: I recommend including as much clear quartz as you can.

★ You can prepare for this activation by getting yourself comfortable and grounding. Breathe a few long deep breaths into your heart then take them into your stomach.

★ Take some time to call in your protection, asking: "Archangel Michael stand in front of me, Archangel Michael stand behind me, above and below me, to my left and to my right."

★ Invoke a beautiful tube of pure white light to surround you, ascending from the Earth and descending from the stars.

★ Allow your body to relax and soften into the ground beneath you, as each breath magnetizes your body deeper into the floor beneath you, into the Earth, into that totally held space.

★ Taking more calming, soothing deep breaths. Focus on the in-breath: through this you can guide your body faster into a sense of deep relaxation, being present but not attached.

★ Bring awareness to all of the crystals on your body from top to bottom, feeling their light and weight one by one and allowing that flow of energy into your body, observing not attaching. View where their coloured rays go.

★ Bring awareness to your third eye, where the clear quartz lies. It starts to shine bright, like a beacon of light that bursts into your third eye chakra through the pathways you have opened and realigned, flowing in like liquid light. It moves through your brain and lights each hemisphere in pure diamond light, moving exactly to where it needs to go. It collects in the centre of your brain in your pineal gland.

★ You imagine not just the quartz's diamond light travelling inside you, but the actual crystal shrinking in your vision and merging into your third eye and travelling through to your pineal gland, exuding a diamond radiance that is felt by all parts of you.

★ This light travels down through you now to the points in your body, energy meridians, nodes and centres that have expanded over the course of the journey, allowing the quartz light to light these areas up.

★ When you observe your body now, it is like a glowing map of source light. You see all the places your body has expanded clearly. The brighter the radiance, the bigger the activation, alignment and re-coding.

★ The quartz replenishes you deeply in light, aligning you to the zero-point field, the pure point of oneness through the elevation of ascension keys in your blueprint. You feel yourself lifting up in this magnificent sphere of light, higher and higher until you transcend consciousness and travel straight to the highest planes of seventh, eighth, ninth, tenth, eleventh and twelfth dimensions of brilliant light. Here, you settle and receive a vision for your crystalline twelve-strand DNA, holding the vision of it in every cell crystallization in the purest emanations of source light. This paves the way for the reconnection.

* We allow the new Earth elemental light council to come close to us, and they and your star family are guides to hold space and your ancestors as we honour your connection and the ancient wisdom you carry. We call all governing light councils and the master cosmos, the divine director and the lords of light and karma to oversee this exchange. We ask them to come in with your earthly and cosmic records to assist us in this release and reclamation of light keys and codes.

* The keys of light within your body that you have been collecting and storing over many millennia are opening now. Your crystalline DNA shifts through your cells and divine templates.

* Your guides begin to tap into your lightbody with golden source light, to release the energetic coding you that you have stored from golden ages: ancient Earth keys of light needed for awakening and accelerating the ascension timelines.

* It spirals from you as ripples of golden light. It downloads stellar activations personal to you and your Earth work, helping you to align with your soul's purpose.

* The crystalline codex of light has been opened within and through you to assist your re-awakening.

* You are held in a multitude of prismatic light and sound, reaching and touching all parts, aspects and blueprints of you, through all timelines. You rise still higher to merge with the source of all, the golden sun above your head.

* Moving through this golden sun, finally complete, you feel yourself release grit and skin, layers of yourself you have grown out of, unwrapping it from your spine, like a caterpillar transforming. Your body emerges as a cosmic golden egg,

crystalline and transparent. You are re-birthing your highest vibrational template, your highest vibrational self. And you feel so much more expanded, so much more connected.

* You breathe in as the Earth breathes in, feeling the Earth below you inhale and contract, and then you exhale as the Earth exhales. You expand in consciousness; you are one.

* Take a moment to feel your expansiveness and how your light touches all around it.

* In this space of receiving joy and breathing in infinite love we are greeted by the smiling faces of our guides, as they come close and circle you, nodding their heads in appreciation. They are your star family, the ascended masters, goddesses, animals, ancestors. They are all here for you.

* You feel a swell of gratitude in your heart and body that washes through you as you allow yourself to fully open to the mysteries of the universe.

Sun setting at Duddo stone circle in Northumberland.

How to Ground Yourself After Activations

This is a little breathing practice to help you ground, anchor and honour the energies after journeys and meditations, as I know the frequencies are high in this book. Each chapter is imbued and encoded with energies to be absorbed. They will be in absolute alignment and harmony with the level of frequency you can hold at this time, so as you come back to the book and do the activations at different stages in your personal development, they will land differently. I always advise people to redo my recorded workshops and crystal courses when they feel wish to, as each time they will receive something different.

* Begin this practice by breathing deeply into your belly, inhaling through your nose, and connecting with all of these loving energies around you. Absorb them, following the flow of energy in your body and acknowledging how good it feels.
* Relaxing your mouth and chin, loosen your lips and let the breath go slowly, exhaling through your mouth.
* Inhale through the nose, feeling the air rush into your nostrils and travel down your diaphragm, expanding your lungs. Take slow, steady, conscious breaths. Breathe in all of the divine experiences and realizations you have come to, while your guides tend to you and make you comfortable.
* Inhale this love, and exhale peace. Continuing in this pattern, bringing yourself back into your body, back home.
* Call all of your energy back into full presence.
* Ground down through golden roots from your heart, becoming a golden tree of life, with your roots growing down

deep and your branches reaching up through your crown to the highest heavens.

★ Send out ripples of gratitude for all there is and the "all" you are connected to through your ever-expanding heart. The end of one journey is the beginning of a next.

"We are the dance of the moon and sun.
We are hope that will never hide.
We are the turning of the tide."

Crystalline Wisdom Resurfacing

It is incredibly important to honour the ancient protectors and the new energies coming into this plane of existence.

While travelling and connecting with the land as I researched this book, I observed a great shift in the crystalline consciousness. The limiting grasp we once had on how we interact with its energies, potential and the energetic grids is really lifting. Specific crystals from Lemuria, Atlantis and the crystal skulls collective are ready to offer more light and frequency to those who are ready. The next wave of children will be encoded with the light needed for more crystal awakening. The reason this is happening is exactly the reason why we are finding new crystals in the Earth: because it is the right time and we are ready.

The divine feminine particularly has been working to release entanglements and programs of control from the womb. The divine feminine's portal of power and creation is bubbling up as it reclaims its power. Many of us are retrieving and healing soul fragmentation that happened in Atlantis when it was lost.

Some of you reading this now are protectors of the Earth and its stones. We have had and continue to have simultaneous moments of existence on many planes at once and many pieces of us are still holding close crystalline energies that we have protected through many years and timelines. The need for us to continue to protect them has gone. This need is an illusion held fast by fears and programming of old. We are being asked to reconnect with those parts of us still serving and protecting on ancient timelines, but your role is fulfilled, your job done and you can release your energy from those sites and sacred spaces, pilgrim routes and temples. There is a great shift at this point in Earth's ascension cycle, a changing of the guards, and as your energy releases from the grid, a crystal, a sacred site, a relic or a scripture and expands somewhere else, a new protector energy will over-light it.

My first experience of this was when I was shown how I was also a young Mayan warrior protecting a large clear crystal skull. I believe it was one of the thirteen that was transported from Atlantis. I was one of many guardians in the inner circle, and I spent most of my life under the Earth, hidden and holding these energies. I was guided down into the Earth by the Great Mother to receive myself. There, in the depths of a step temple, I found myself on guard, still at the doorway, taking my role very seriously. Behind me in the inner chamber of the Earth was a great and very active clear crystal skull, radiating so much golden light that it lit up the space. I knew instinctively that my work was done and that I needed to let go. Whatever crystalline consciousness existed in this space was safe and where it needed to be. There were many before me there to watch over it. So I reconnected with that fragment of my soul, and once I had shown him love he began to accept that he could move on. He turned into light and swirled into my heart. From that moment, with his energy moving through me, I remembered more and more of my past and my connection to the crystal skulls.

There was another moment like this when I was holding a retreat with a group of women in Glastonbury in England, at the abbey. We were standing in the crypt dedicated to Joseph of Arimathea, and when we placed our hands on that cold stone I saw it unlock and open, and from the centre a chalice rose up with a blue flame burning bright inside it. I heard the spirit of the place say, "Those present here must release their energies from this point in the grids to free the light." And as I held that intent for us and explained what I was seeing, the blue flame leapt from the chalice and dispersed.

My last memorable experience of this was in Mexico. There is a beautiful feminine temple site there at Muyil, and it was one of the star temples where I connected with this release and changing of the guards. As I walked up the temple I felt a rumble through the ground, and sensed it was a place of great significance. The whole place was glowing with pink light, as though it were a focus for the pink ray of divine love. I tapped certain stones with my clear quartz and witnessed something magical. Once again the stones started to unlock, opening piece by piece, and in the centre point was the most magnificent field of love, radiating from a very large rose quartz crystal skull. The pink light got brighter, and around it were three otherworldly beings. They were tall and looked as if they were made of diamond, with elongated skulls and feathers all the way down from where their ears would have been to the floor. They felt like Mayan timekeepers. I was there to witness their energies release from the site and was asked to return there with others, to take crystal skulls and to anchor seventh-dimensional frequency templates at the site. I have done this three times now. The first time, I took a group of thirteen women, and brought along a large rose quartz skull. They each brought one too, so we had a council of thirteen because the Mayans believed that thirteen was a lucky number. The last two occasions each occurred at potent astrological moments – eclipses – and these were totally unknown to me when I booked the trip.

So I leave this message with you: the protectors must release their hold in order for the new to come in. Where we release our hold, the grid expands, and the influx of energies deepens. This is what is being asked of you: to connect with those pieces of yourself that are still protecting the pockets of Lemurian crystals under the Earth in the tunnel networks, and those parts of you splintered on Atlantean timelines still serving and protecting the temples out of honour, guilt, shame or fear. Those of you who are crystal skull guardians must meet them and ask them to let go. Your role is fulfilled, your job is done and was done to the best of your ability. You are loved and the Earth is so grateful for you.

The Crystals

I am a crystal guardian through many lifetimes, realms and planes, from my remembrance of my past in Lemuria creating Lemurian seed crystals from my diamond heart, to gridding temple space with master record keepers in Atlantis. My wisdom has come from my reconnection to my priestess past, in the lineages of goddesses Isis and Magdalene; I connect so fully with the plant and alchemy realms and consciously with the stones and their spirits, especially crystal skulls and the universal consciousness they channel as cosmic streams of information. The medicine of "Stone and Bone" is in my ancestral blood on this Earth walk and many others.

It feels right to start this journey of the stones with you with the protective and deeply holding energies of labradorite. It is a stone steeped in stories, with some that you may not have heard before. It is a stone of the stars, of heaven and Earth, and born of both. I ask that you receive these stories in the loving intent with which I scribed them. Thank you for journeying with me.

"You feel a swell of gratitude in your heart and body that washes through you as you allow yourself to fully open to the mysteries of the universe."

Earthing grid of polychrome jasper, red rock,
iron in quartz, aragonite, copper and citrine
to connect with for grounding and anchoring
the wisdom as you read these words.

Hand-carved shaman in Labradorite, the stone
that initiated me into its mysteries.

Labradorite

I have always loved Labradorite's mystery, feeling her voice as a wise woman who whispers in riddles. She has been my most elusive – and in times of need my most generous – healer, showing up at times of great change to shepherd me through conflict. She's the high-vibrational honey to the third eye, and when I move through moments of difficulty, she sees that inner struggle and applies her energy to the wound to let the light in.

Labradorite amplifies and shines a light on our interconnectivity. When you hold a piece of Labradorite, remember that its wisdom has been in the hands of many protectors through time. When I hold it, I see my hands shift into the hands of the ancients, changing shape, colour and texture. I feel what they feel. Just as when you speak to one tree, all trees feel your love as they are all connected, all of the stones are connected through the crystalline grid. The crystalline grid is a matrix of light energy in the Earth: you could visualize it as a spider's web of glistening diamond light that connects all crystals above and below the Earth. It feels a lot like the mycelium (mushroom) networks. Each crystal has a unique story, with incredible guardian energies held withing it. The ancients speak through the stones. We just have to listen.

It is said that Labradorite was first brought to the attention of Western science in the late 1700s – 1770 to be exact – in Labrador, Newfoundland, Canada, by Moravian missionaries. We can feel from the guardians that it is much older. It has been referenced in legends by older Inuit tribes. One of these legends has it that the Northern Lights were once stuck inside rocks on the Canadian coast until a brave warrior freed many of them by hitting the rocks with a spear. The rocks that were not hit still have those Northern Lights within them, the cause of the beautiful iridescent quality Labradorite possesses.

Wounds are Labradorite's speciality: she likes to offer her light to heal and soothe warrior wounds, past-life echoes and imprints. These rise for her to heal. She offers the visual of her cracking you open, and her light seeps out in sound and moves into your hands. She loves to support hands-on healers. Her deep wish is to support the sensitivity in you, and her light will move in through all layers of the emotional, mental and physical field to the wounds in your body.

Working With Labradorite's Medicine

Labradorite is a space holder for pain, and for talking to the resistance that lives in the body. You can feel this through her voice (see page 63). She does this by not wearing things down with talk and false hope, but just observes, listening to its needs and then letting it run out. "We stand gently holding," she says: it's this safe space she brings to explore alternate levels of consciousness and planes of existence that you travel through. She brings fluidity and ease of movement through these in-between states, with a safe landing back into your body and present moment.

Labradorite offers us the beautiful image of the Earth cracking open at the seams, bursting with Labradorite light: a beautiful blue, turquoise and golden glow that shimmers with an otherworldly quality. Her medicine is for the third eye, but because her colours flash blue, turquoise and green they can also resonate with the throat and heart and she supports the grounding of wisdom streams through your higher chakras to activate your third eye. She will expand this energy centre with light and dissolve past-life fears as you witness them.

It has been said that Labradorite will open your third eye, but you are mistaken for thinking just placing it there will bring an opening. Everyone is different and some have more past-life trauma in their third eye than others, especially those with past lives as seers and divinators. We have to connect and work with accepting Labradorite's sometimes tough words and challenging energy. She will bring forward past-life visions with ease and grace because she is a strong visionary stone. Known to strengthen and connect the third eye channels to all energy systems and pathways within you, she works to support energetic upgrades on the eyes, the windows of the soul. I have often been guided by this stone to cool two Labradorite flat tumble stones with ice and place them on closed eyelids of those who have "seen" too much pain and hardship. They soothe the eyes and connecting muscles on the physical spirit and mental layers of the aura.

I had a special experience when I met a large Labradorite carving of the goddess Hathor, the cosmic mother, famed in ancient Egypt as the mother goddess of creation, creativity, fertility, dance, music and sensuality. The stone's mystic, deep and ever-unfolding energy surrounded me and called me to her. I gazed into its carved eyes and she simply asked me: "Are you ready?" With that I placed my third eye to hers, which felt natural and apt for a stone that activates the third eye. She opened a portal of powerful light into my third eye, which bore through me and cracked open the back of my skull with light, reflecting the visual Labradorite offers you of "cracking open". Then she took me through liminal space, as she is a journeying stone, holding many doorways open to cosmic consciousness. Here we met in council with the goddess as they unfolded around me. That experience was the catalyst for my deeper initiation from the goddess, into the mysteries of the rose and universal heart teachings.

This experience beautifully highlights Labradorite's grace and ability for self-discovery, awakening your awareness to the universal consciousness plane, deepening your intuition and psychic abilities, including clairvoyance, telepathy, prophecy, access to the Akashic plane and records of Amenti. There are many energies waiting to connect with you and this stone opens those doorway for them, and for you.

One of the joint themes we all share is a feeling of "shame" that can be stored in various places in the body and lightbody, and more often than not is inherited through our ancestors and mother line. Through my work I often witness a lot of shame in the bones, womb and adrenals of the body, and it is always

Labradorite who steps forward to assist a gentle discovery and release of this shame. It can calm the harsh voice within the negative thought patterns we replay: our inner critic that goads us into all of these feelings around our self-worth.

The shamans and healers over many ages have also embraced Labradorite as a stone of magic and universal knowledge and guidance. It is a powerful protector of the mineral kingdom, and it prevents energy leaking (anyone tapping into your energy and draining you). I love that it creates a strong shield around you by strengthening your energies from within; its song is of freedom, as it helps you explore, free of restraints and conditioning, allowing you to journey freely through many planes of existence, while it protects you with a gentle and high frequency that does not hold your spirit still.

The Ancestors' Medicine: The Red-Painted People

The Red-Painted People lived between 7,000–9,000 years ago, hunting and fishing along the rivers from New England to Labrador. They are a mysterious tribe and not very much is written or known about them, so I feel honoured to sit with them and learn, as the Red-Painted People have been visiting me in my dreams. Here, I forge a deeper connection with Labradorite's medicine, as they have been working with it for over a thousand years. Before them it was worked with by older Inuit tribes. Inuit legend claims that Labradorite is the frozen fire of the Aurora Borealis fallen to the earth, shimmering its mystical light that separates the waking world from unseen realms. This stone helps us walk between these realms. The Red-Painted People repeatedly take me to their land in New England and parts of North America, where they tell me that they are humble hunter gatherers, who care for their community. They are the water keepers and way showers of the continent, forging new pathways. They understand the ways of the waters and are in tune with all of the water's inhabitants who they commune with. It is the Red-Painted People who have come forward to initiate me into the mysteries of Labradorite as a powerful Earth energy for change and opening.

First Labradorite Vision

I am welcomed into their tribe in a ceremony by the river. The elder females took time to grind the red ochre paint they are named after with heated and ground rocks and roots, saliva and white-tailed deer blood that has been caught for the ceremony. They use the bones of the deer to stir the mixture, which is a sacred process with their land. One female elder made the paste: she had this special role.

My place is to sit by the river and connect with the water, because for the Red-Painted People, everything revolved around this source of life, and in this place the spirit of the Great Mother is celebrated. They dressed me in a simple deerskin pelt, and I am left in stillness to connect with the land. As the air danced through my hair and the sound of the river bustles by my side, I was visited by the animal spirits and protectors of that tribe. A guardian trout spirit jumped up to greet me – a symbol of wisdom, knowledge, strength and fertility to the tribe. They revere this spirit as a protector and guardian. Many birds joined me, of all different sizes, wanting me to know that the birds worked closely with the Red-Painted People.

The tribe showed me their delicate place within the ecosystem here and how they worked closely with the waters and water beings to bring rest to unrest, peace to friction, and harmony and love to the cells of all. The elders gather around me, making whistling and clicking sounds with their mouths, whistling for the bird spirits, clicking bones together and stamping their feet on the Earth. The red paste is brought forward in a simple stone vessel with leaves. It's bright red, like blood; they say it is the blood of the Earth. And the Earth is initiating me as one of hers.

The elder mother who created this paste stands in front of me and holds my face firmly with both hands under my chin, so firm that it's slightly uncomfortable. She is asking for change, she is asking me to pledge myself to bring change for the Earth and its inhabitants. She speaks of a day that rivers will dry up and crops will fail and animals will have no food. She is concerned for this day. She takes a palm full of paste and rubs it over my left cheek, then over my right. Then she holds her hands over my eyes, chanting:

"May Mother Earth receive you.
May Mother Earth hold you.
May Mother Earth forgive you.
May we be humble and serve the Earth ways."

She traces dots and lines over my face in layers, though this can't be seen as my face is now completely red and the paste is drying thick in the sun. But I feel them etched in: the energy leaves its imprints in my field. The elder is an alchemist working with Mother Earth's cycles and her waters. In that moment she is the embodiment of the Earth. All the while the community witness and sing. I have joined this small community at a time they are starting to disperse, travel and branch out to explore new territory. Before they move they show me their connection to Labradorite – a journey stone and an energy that bridges the Earth and the stars. They are an embodiment of the Earth and Labradorite is of the stars connecting us with cosmic consciousness and expansion.

The Red-Painted People are the protectors of the Earth and were brought to finding this stone because only they understand the precious balance between Earth and stars that needs to be embodied as we expand. In being so grounded in the Earth they have the capacity to bring in high star frequencies. They understand the way Labradorite expands consciousness and takes us up the cosmic consciousness planes of existence. They say:

"To hold Labradorite is to hold a piece of the stars."

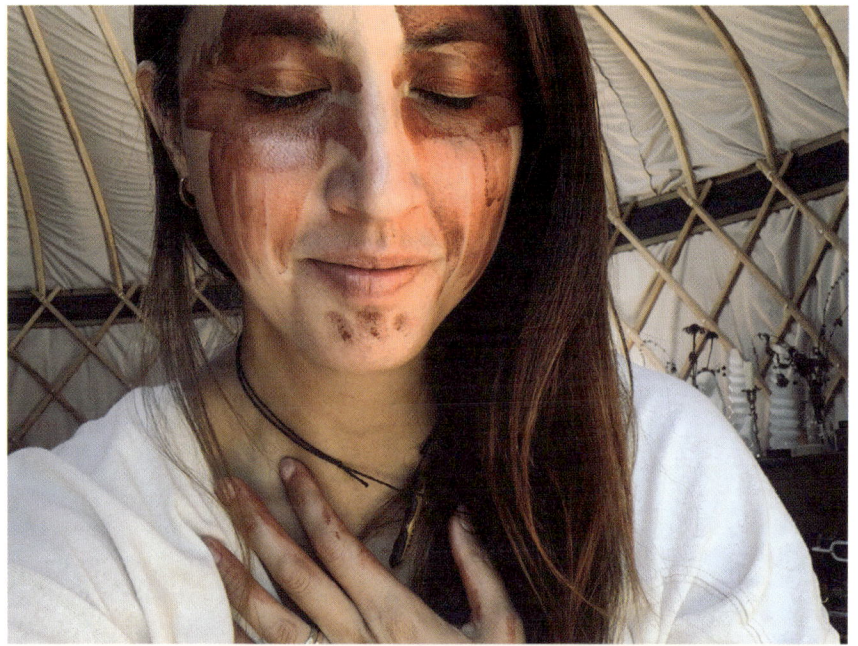

In initiation with the spirit of the Red-Painted People.

Labradorite has been called the "Temple of the Stars" by many over time, bringing the light of other planetary beings to the soul of the person working with it. It bridges otherworldly energies to the Earth plane, bringing races of similar frequencies together to heal soul groups and tribes. It holds a strong "Vega" signature and those who connect with their Lyran aspects will really resonate with this stone, or feel a push to work with it now as it will realign and awaken that ancestry line within them to bring healing.

Second Labradorite Vision

The next time the Red-Painted People visit me in my dream time a young male hunter called Nha ta appears holding a spear with a rough piece of Labradorite on the end of it. He strikes it on the Earth, its blue light erupts and creates a vortex of light. He takes my hand, and my hand is not my own. I am a young girl of about seven years old. He leads me to the river bed as we skip through time. Many birds join us on the journey, flying beside us and a deep stirring in my heart is followed by an incredible love for this Earth. These people, my family, adore the Earth and are one with the Earth and animal spirits: I feel it in them. I'm sitting in a memory that feels so real, as if it's part of me. This hunter is my brother, and he's washing my face with care before I am shown how to gather the roots and rocks for their red paste. He holds my eyes as the elder had in the ceremony before, and the circle of time is presented to me once more, he is the elder, and I am the grandmother making the paste and painting the face of those around me; the initiation is being passed on through these words.

A healing energy is transferred through his hands from his heart. Instantly my eyes look and feel like Labradorite. I can see and feel my multi-dimensionality, flashes of all I have been, and the feeling of everything happening at once.

I somehow know that this Labradorite tool he has is a powerful connection to the universe. The tenderness of the moment softens my heart to tears; I feel such love in this space from these ancestors. This feels important, the wish and need to carry forward these words of the Earth and stars through Labradorite, through the Red-Painted People.

I learned that this red paint was not reserved just for burial, but was for ceremony and communion with the Earth, as this tribe are shapeshifters and divinators of the Earth. One day we will find our way back to the Earth. The Red-Painted People know it, and this is why they leave their blessings with Labradorite, so we may follow the path home, as it lights and connects the way.

Third Labradorite Vision

Another day, I met the Red-Painted People at the waters where they were making fishing nets and communing with the trout spirit. They told me a legend about a spirit called Akura, which tells of how they came to work with Labradorite.

One day the tribe's men were walking down by the river to go fishing. They saw three cranes fly overhead. It was rare to see one crane, but three: this was an omen. They heard the cries of a young girl who they found at the side of the river. As they approach her they notice she is crying glowing blue tears of light, and as the light falls to the floor it solidifies into Labradorite. The men sit with her, captivated by these shiny stones that reflect the heavens to them, and she stops crying and witnesses their wonder. She picks up the Labradorite and offers them to the tribe's men in exchange for shelter, food and warmth. They take her back to their community where she lives with them, and finds a home with them. She no longer cries tears of sorrow but tears of joy at experiencing love and community with strangers that become family.

The day she joined the tribe, the Red-Painted People became protectors of this star energy. The young star girl, Akura, became one of them and her star wisdom was passed on through the tribe. The Red-Painted People were offered infinite wisdom that the Earth had not seen before, because they were humble Earth people who lived in harmony with nature. After this story the ancestors said:

"Don't you see that you are the star child, come again to tell the stories of the people."

 ## Red Ochre Paint

The ceremony of the red ochre paint is something I now work with physically by way of honouring the Red-Painted People. The first time I painted it on my face with my hands, I held Labradorite in my heart, and with it the stars as well as the Earth below my feet. The grandmothers came close, they sang to me and clicked around my crown, impressing their energies through my hands and I cried because their energy was such a loving embrace.

They asked me:

"Why do you cry? Our messages may be serious in the
Earth ways, but our song through the stone is one of joy
and reverence; we sing to the soul on its transitions, and
the red paint honours their blood, as all blood is one."

I feel the love they have for the Earth through them, through
their hands and hearts.

They say to me:

"You are Akura. It is the water of life that connects us through
galaxies and stars; all tears are sweet; all tears are one."

Red ochre is the world's first red paint: it is clay pigmented by
hematite, a reddish mineral that contains oxidized iron. Having
that level of iron and hematite on my face, painted vertically
down with two hands from my eyebrows, was extremely
grounding. It brought my energy down into my body from my
higher chakras and into my feet. Then I used two hands (as I had
been shown) to paint it horizontally from left to right across my
closed eyes, and layered on dots as the grandmothers guided
me. I am in awe at the deep initiations of Labradorite. I am
feeling the ancestors as me, as they are you; all is one.

My journey with Labradorite has been so sacred, and more
than I could ever imagine. I don't want her teachings to end
and in many ways they will not, because now I am marked
with them. They are in me and part of me. But still a sadness
creeps over me to think I have to leave these people I have felt
one with. Labradorite helps us strip back the separation, and
knowing that that connection is always there, never lost. I had
never felt such a strong connection with Labradorite as the one

I feel now. Dedicating this time to sit with a stone's ancestors will surely do this to you too. Holding Labradorite now, I feel a belonging. I feel I am part of something great and vast, and I feel the greatness of those around me. I can trace the story lines back through the keepers of Labradorite, and peace flows through me like its blue turquoise light. We must open ourselves to look through the eyes of Labradorite, with the spirit of Akura, who sees the stars and Earth as one.

Before I journeyed with the Red-Painted People I had read nothing about them, as with anything I like to go in and receive with no preconceived notions, projections or ideas of others. Allowing myself to do some reading after, I found one thing that really made me smile as it nodded to their mystery. They had the skills and knowledge to build sailing vessels thousands of years before cultures to the east, making them among the world's first known voyagers. They also created tools and techniques for fishing to make hunting for large fish on the open water possible, contributing to humankind's environmental awareness,

Labradorite
and sea coal.

pushing the boundaries around what is possible. All of a sudden their sacred understanding of the trout spirits and the birds they mentioned so often made sense: the animals as well as the land were their teachers. I would like to think the spirit of Akura who taught them many things in return for the wisdom of the stars.

The indigenous cultures' folklore is peppered with stories of beings from the Pleiades being their ancestors, founding their cultures and ceremony, so an otherworldly visitor like Akura does not seem so strange. Cherokee, Lakota and Dakota legend teaches that they originated from the Pleiades, and the Navajo call the Pleiadian star cluster the "Sparkling Suns".

Even though they are gone their spirit lives on through these words: Blessed be to all the ancestors of the Red-Painted People. We are truly grateful for your love.

Meeting Labradorite

* Stand barefoot on the Earth, holding a piece of Labradorite, turning it in your palm, noticing its edges, texture and the way the light dances off it. Call forward its protectors and guides.
* Feel the Red-Painted People come close to hold you in their light, the Inuit elders and all fish and bird spirits drop in as you breathe. Connect with the spirit of the waters and the rivers around you, feel them flowing through you.
* Feel a transfer of light from the Labradorite into your heart and hands, and all other places ready to receive it.
* Feel the Earth below you through your feet. Allow yourself to drop into the Earth now and into the crystalline grid of diamond

light, which appears to light a delicate diamond crystal spider web.

★ The Labradorite moves into your heart and becomes part of you, with it all the wisdom of the ancestors who held it and worked with you coming into your heart too. You may see or feel your eyes turn into Labradorite now, feeling its glow infusing your eyes and third eye.

★ Feel its blue and turquoise glow move through you, scanning your body from top to bottom, identifying places that need a shake-up, rejuvenating or rest.

★ Allow its energy to surge and search your lightbody through all layers, and follow its flow of light, not attaching to them, but just allowing.

★ Breathe deeper, welcoming it fully and allowing it into your body, heart, mind and soul.

★ Invite the Red-Painted People into your heart and allow the grandmothers to paint your face and sing to you in celebrations as you come back to the ancient Earth roots.

★ When you are ready, gently open your eyes and ask these questions. You may wish to grab a notebook and pen and write down what you feel.

What do my ancestors and the Red-Painted People wish me to know? What do they wish me to see? Could they show me where there is imbalance in my systems?
What can I do to bring more of a balance within?
What can I do to bring more of a balance to the Earth?

"What you seek is not always what you wish to find. When you turn over a stone in the river, the minnows will dart away, the bottom dwellers will burrow under the sand and grit and you expose more layers of life, but does that life wish to be exposed? Some beings enjoy the comfort of the shadows and the dark; it is safe for them and it may be all they are used to.

As a human walking the Earth at this time, it is your responsibility to turn over the stones and to dig deeper, but you might not always find what you expect, and that which you do find might not wish to be found. There will be resistance within and around you, and my light is one of "digging deep", searching the darker corners of the soul, creating an invitation to those parts of you that feel so comfortable under the stone. When I shine a light on them they may shy away, run, hide, they may even kick and shout within you. But just as a child who needs attention, focus and love, they will tire in the end. We stand gently holding, and we must keep shining that light on the dark spaces. Within you and within humanity, and on the Earth."

Labradorite

Protective crystal grid with different forms of Obsidian:
snowflake Obsidian, Apache Tears Obsidian, quartz with
tourmaline, clear quartz, black kynite, pearl and pearlite.

Obsidian

Black is a colour of authority in almost every culture in the world: a colour of mystery and secrets, commanding respect and a sense of power. It is a colour that blocks and protects, speaking to an inner primal part of us.

In my *Songs of the Stones Oracle* deck, Obsidian's energy wished to pair with that of the Jaguar, who walks between worlds, attached but unattached, of the world, but not in the world. There is a balanced dance of union she weaves, protecting you through changes. And her energies reflect that of Obsidian. There are many variations of Obsidian: sheen Obsidian in silver and gold and rainbow, spider web, snowflake, mahogany and fire Obsidian being the rarest. Each holds a slightly different vibration and a different element of support, but all have these underlying core values.

Obsidian is a crystal that for years has made me uneasy, unsure about the depth of healing it would expose, so much so that I avoided it completely. It is a very powerful and ancient volcanic glass, formed of a strong love and connection to life, death and creation. On Earth it takes on the role of a very protective crystal, sought after as a protective amulet to carry or wear to provide grounding and safety. I see the many tribes that know its potency and add to the fiercely protective feeling this stone radiates. It evokes the need to protect, to serve and to honour its depth.

Obsidian has a rich history with the Mayas and shamans of Native American tribes. As a hand-crafted tool it is found in the earliest Earth temples, as it is chipped easily to reveal very sharp edges. I reserve my shard of Obsidian for intense lightbody clearing as a psychic scalpel to cut away very deep attachments and entities from the aura, and it's excellent for helping to remove deep trauma. Holding black Obsidian will cast a moving black shield form around your aura that will scan and process the energies around you before they connect with the inner layers of your aura, and block out any negative or harmful energies around you. But its energy runs much deeper than that: working with black Obsidian is a relationship of complete trust and surrender, and it asks of the highest levels of trust. It is serious in its work and asks you to be the same. Do not underestimate this stone's potency: it must be revered and worked with care. Obsidian's medicine finds you when you are teetering on the edge of the void space to show you that expanse: the dark space where all is created. Its energy is masculine, but it understands the need for balance within the feminine aspect to penetrate the cosmic mother's womb energy.

The ancients call Obsidian the stone of many uses. It was used for initiation rites in Atlantis by the first tribes of RA, a collective of star frequencies that brought a vast amount of crystal frequency to the Earth through its teachings of oneness. These tribes worked with the stone to anchor new star templates into the Earth as it pins new currents into the light grids. It was a focus stone for them, something that could direct energy in a sharp and clear manner. It was frequently used by the priestess of Isis in ceremonies and rituals. Originating from Atlantis, Goddess Isis carries the divine mother template, mother of all, a high priestess and carrier of the rose lineage womb codes of unity from ancient Egypt. Here their devotional temple arts worked with the energies of stones such as ruby, Obsidian and garnet. Its ability to "draw out", purify, purge and detoxify was revered by the priestess who scried with this stone in ancient Egypt, due to its highly reflective properties, which uncover truths hidden deep within, and the hidden wisdom of the gods. It enhanced their visionary capacity by reflecting only true light to them. Its power as a portal opener and an

"in-between" world stone that opened the third eye. They understood its mystic and magic ways and brought it into ritual and initiation, working with slabs of black Obsidian that the initiate would lie on to draw out energies from the lightbody.

Harnessing the energies of the stones for protection.

At this point in the ascension cycle, Obsidian holds a strong light to support us in cutting away false grids and matrices within the Earth and mental field of the collective field. Its focus can be drawn to identifying false light and support the falling away of agendas which do not serve the Earth's evolutionary process. Obsidian is a gateway stone into the deepest levels of cellular memory within you because it is one of the most ancient stones used by many cultures and civilizations across the world, and because of that it holds all ancestral imprints like a library. It has the frequency to untangle neuro pathways in the brain so that you can re-wire yourself and deprogram, just as it deprograms and directs currents through the Earth grids.

I have had a lot of time to sit with Obsidian, especially when travelling through Yucatán where it's found in abundance and used by the Maya. It presents the initiation of death, unlike any other stone you can work with. Obsidian reminds us that, "Death is a doorway into the eternal."

The Mayas understand that death is to befriended. Many of their rituals and ceremonies centre around death and rebirth because that is everything. From the Temazcal (sweat lodge) ceremony that they take part in to cleanse, purify and rebirth themselves, to their belief in sacrifice, it is an honour to give your blood back to the land, and to become one with the Earth and add to its fertility. They would cut themselves with Obsidian blades to let their blood onto the Earth. In our modern society this could be viewed as barbaric. I am guilty of that feeling. As a deeply feeling person, when visiting the stones at a temple complex called Coba in Tulum, I sat with the stones and found myself feeling it all, and saying sorry for all the bloodshed this place had seen, to which the ancestors and spirit of place answered to me in a very commanding voice, "Do not be sorry, it was honourable and they chose that path." It was such a beautiful reminder of how we project on sites and land with our own ideas when really we have no idea of their position, circumstances or agreements of contracts. And so putting to the side all my preconceived ideas of how Obsidian was worked with in the past, I quieted my mind and asked the crystals to show me the truth.

They took me to a hall of mirrors, all made of Obsidian, all facing me, and asked me:

"What do you see?"

I saw my reflection as I focused on the first Obsidian mirror. I was looking sad, eyes bloodshot from crying, and I was my younger self, holding a teddy that I didn't recognize in my right hand, and with my left hand I was pulling my hair in despair. I questioned myself: is this what I wanted to see or was this real? Obsidian said:

"It is real to you. That is all that matters. I only present you with the reality you have woven through your being. Everyone's reality is different and can change every day. You shape and mould your experience and we are gazing at a reality and template you wove when you were five years old. One where you said 'yes' to loneliness, and decided to torment yourself with this untruth, until now. I show you this because it is time to let it go. This template and story is not true, and only now are you ready to see this. You do not have to feel lonely, because you are not alone. You have said yes to unconditional love, and when you do that

and see how much you deserve, you can free yourself of so much false baggage you have been carrying. You cannot be happy until 'she' is happy.

"But we need to show that to this version of you so she can free herself.

"What would it take for you to feel whole and included?"

Even though I have done this many times before, over and over, it has not been enough. I don't know if we can ever show our younger selves enough love, but we have to keep going. I knew that I needed to show her the ways I am loved now, so I brought in the loves of my life and I showed her how they love me unconditionally, and that their love was not limited and extended to her now. She dropped the teddy and looked at her hands, as if seeing them for the first time. She let out a roar, and energy burst from her hands. She jumped out of the Obsidian mirror to hug me. I asked her if we could let go of this, and located where I had stored this template in my body, scanning my mental and then emotional body for its imprints. I then let it go knowing that I did not have to feel lonely again because I had found something that makes me feel whole. When I looked back at the Obsidian mirror in front of me there was just the glow of black nothingness, and she gazed at it with me, smiling. Looking around this space I looked at all the mirrors reflecting at me and I saw me, as I present now. I looked happy, content and peaceful. I felt strong and self-assured. I was proud of the woman I saw in front of me. She had everything she needed and she looked happy.

Obsidian said:

"The records of remembrance are always open to you through me, no matter how hard or painful the story you have committed to. I hold you in strong reassurance that although this is hard now, better days are coming. This is one thread of hundreds of stories that you play out."

We sink into the story that Obsidian is a fierce protector, and that feels good. It's a story we are fed through books. But it is so much more. It is a shadow mirror because for it to be able to protect and hold you it would make sense that it sees and understands the deepest shadows it serves to protect or initiate you from. And that is often yourself. It's not anything outside of you; it's the false narratives you have fed yourself. It shows you the shadows within you because it knows that the greatest healing has to come from looking internally. So if you have something that you don't feel you can shift – a feeling, a worry or fear – look to Obsidian to help you locate it within your psyche. Stand in the hall of Obsidian mirrors and ask it to support you in your realization. It will present you with what you need to see and help you look through it to the truth.

I have worked with the Obsidian mirror with people to focus on bringing forward their inner child wounding and past life pain. Every experience is interesting and of course different: there are many who stand in front of the Obsidian mirror and see nothing, and that is not wrong. It's just that something is blocked or not ready to be seen, and it is a process of going back to access different things depending on where you are in your healing journey.

Rhodochrosite central stone to open the heart, opalite, Obsidian tumble stones, clear quartz and pyrite.

Connecting With Obsidian

For this meditation, hold some Obsidian and place it wherever feels comfortable. You can also take some time to gaze at the Obsidian crystal grid I have constructed opposite (page 72) and feel its energies pool into the centre point and infuse your lightbody and chakras with its light.

* Before we start, create a high-frequency protective sphere of diamond rainbow light around you that seals above your head and below your feet.
* Call to you the energies of Obsidian by welcoming its flow of energy into your heart from the grid. Let it flow around your body, noticing where it goes.
* With each breath you breathe in its energy deeper to your being.
* Its energy wants to dig, unearth and open parts of you. You notice where it settles in your body it offers solidity, stability, grounding and protection to your lower chakras.
* Once it has infused and attuned to your lightbody and you feel its light holding you, call on the ancestral energies of Obsidian. Its guardian and protectors come close to surround you now.
* You notice Obsidian is sweeping its energy over you from the crown and out through all seven layers of your aura, to locate anything that does not belong. This grid attends to support the removal of any devices, imprints and holographic inserts through the sacral and lightbody and/or any devices connected through, in or around you and those in your soul group.
* A portal in the Earth beneath you opens and the guardians of Obsidian appear by your side in light to guide you down into

a cave of Obsidian. As you move down this tunnel deep into the Earth beneath you start to see black shards of crystal in the walls, reflecting the light back at you.

★ You come to an inner chamber of black Obsidian mirrors. Standing in the centre of these black mirrors, reflecting back at you in a circle, you fix your gaze on the Obsidian mirror in front of you, willing it to call forward your shadows. Ask Obsidian to show you any shadows or any neglected parts of you that need to be healed.

★ The spirit of Obsidian speaks to you. "What do you see?" You see your reflection in the Obsidian mirror.

★ It shows you the version of you that you need to free. Whatever you see in the mirror, offer it love and compassion.

★ Ask it to present you with the truth of your being. Sit with it and listen. Thank its guardians and energies when you feel the teaching is complete.

Offerings of love to the earth, flowers and tobacco, after digging for Obsidian.

Apache Tears Obsidian

There are so many stories and legends around crystals being formed by tears. In Greek mythology it is said that opals were formed from Zeus' joyful tears, after winning the battle against the Titans. The ancient Greeks believed amethyst originated from the tears of the god of wine, Dionysus, and could help with sobriety, so they drank wine from amethyst-studded cups. In ancient Japan, it was believed that pearls were created from the tears of angels, mermaids and other mythical beings. The ancient Persians said pearls were the tears of the gods, and the ancient Greeks believed they were formed when Aphrodite emerged from the sea and released tears of joy. Native American folklore says that the rain came after a long drought and the people cried with relief, their tears merged with the waters and became turquoise. I believe this is because tears are the purest expression of love, and crystals reflect this expression of pure love, that help us move with joy, love, pain and all in between. They are also created in a pure sense, from a moment of elemental alchemy within the Earth, and some from the love of the stars (tektites) that are teachers and guides to bring us back to the purest templates and version of ourselves, as the Earth herself is perfect. I had not thought much of crystals' connection to tears until the story of the tears of Akura reminded me of a tale I have heard before of tears turning into precious stones. This legend is centred around the Apache Tears stone, a type of Obsidian volcanic glass only found in the historical territory of the Apache tribe, in the American southwest and northern Mexico.

The pearlite mine in Arizona at sunset.

The Pinal Apache Ancestors

Legend says that the Pinal Apaches in Arizona state had had many raids on their settlement, so to protect the tribe they moved on to a place they thought they were safe, a large rock called Big Picacho, but the US cavalry had followed their tracks and ambushed them. In the first round of shots fifty Apache warriors died and the remaining 25 retreated to the edge of the cliff and chose to fall to their death. The Apache women gathered at the cliff's edge to mourn their loved ones. Their sadness was overwhelming and they wept for a moon. It is said that as the tears fell to the bottom of the cliff the Great Father embedded them into the black stones there. When you hold an Apache Tears stone to the light, it is said that you can see a translucent tear of the Apache in this black Obsidian. I have held this story close for years hoping the right pieces of Apache Tears will find me form their land, holding their stories.

Their story is one of fierce love for the land and its creatures, and a mourning of the tribe when their guardianship was let go of, through force. Three of the ancestral guardian spirits of this stone, the Pinal Apache, come forward with so much love for the Earth as they share their wisdom:

"One can never fully let go of your love for the land you lived on. You are never separated. Just as humans discover they are not separate from the whole, you are symbiotically linked with all things. The land is woven into you and it becomes part of your song. Every plant, leaf, animal and insect you have an interaction with becomes part of your heart, just as your energy becomes one with theirs. In your body you have a vast system of stored frequency, not just of the stones and rocks but of the plants and animals you have interacted with. Everything leaves an imprint.

"Pay attention to the land you live on. Tend to her, listen to her breathe: she breathes with you, she responds to your loving touch and thoughts.

"You are of the land, in the land, with the land.

"Think of your footprint across the Earth, all the Earth you have connected with, touched, walked and climbed. There is land you have lived on before that you come back to, many times not knowing why, but listening to the call. It calls you back because it knows you, and needs you. Wherever you find yourself on this planet, it is for a reason, and you have the opportunity to hold vast amounts of light to pass to the Earth if you choose to.

"You are a traveller of the cosmos bridging energies from near and far to exchange, replenish and release into the Earth. All of your imprints are left, every step, so consider your steps and tread lightly with reverence for her, and all the ways she holds you without question."

To close this brief exchange the three Apache elders that gathered around me offered me a gift made of the Earth: a ceremonial peace pipe made of clay, strung with three turkey feathers, each symbolizing a teaching that they would impart over time and demonstrating their commitment to honour the Earth ways. I had officially been welcomed to the fire to sit with them when the time presented itself.

First Obsidian Vision

It felt important to connect with this land and the ancestors' voices through the stones at the source; although we can connect with any energy by taking ourselves there, I needed my feet on the soil. So I made it my mission to travel there.

I found the canyon the legend is centred around in Superior, Arizona and went on an adventure to listen to the stories of the stones. On the way up we hit pockets of energies next to ancient settlements, holding voices of elders singing, and women speaking to their children, and spirals of pain that the land had held onto like echoes. It was walking past one of these ancient cave settlements that the first Apache tribe elder appeared with a smile.

My worlds often weave through the 3D to the 5D, bridging the past, present and future through my vision, and although I was at the midpoint of the canyon, and the cave was below, I had travelled there energetically to be with this elder. He had a wolf by his side with ice-blue eyes. He motioned for me to come into the cave with him. I noticed a braid in his hair with a single turkey feather; he nodded at me, unpicked his hair and handed me the feather. Feeling it was right to offer him something from me and my world, I handed him a beech seed pod, as they are something I carry to offer my wishes to the Earth. He received it with warmth and intrigue, and showed it to the wolf who sniffed it, and the elder then placed it in his heart.

We walked into the cave, and as we did I could see many ancestral faces staring back at me, taking form on the stone walls. The red rocks here in Arizona really hold a fire and ancestral wisdom to tune in to.

We arrived at the fire and he was making a warm drink for us, which he insisted we drink first before we talk. I could already feel somehow that this lesson would involve scrying, for the way the rocks shapeshifted in a fluid motion across the surface of the cave, and the way the water in the pot was boiling, I could see images shifting on the surface: scenes of his tribe, children playing happily, men hunting, women braiding fabric. He knew what I was watching and said:

"Superior", the canyon I connected
with the Apache Tears legend.

"All of nature offers us the opportunity to 'see' the memories of the past, present and future, the ripples in the water, the sun on a stone, the wind blowing through a tree. Reflecting on nature, with nature, you can tap into the infinite all. It's all talking to you. My people knew what was to come, and to pass for this Earth, the land knows, all is in perfect order. There is a pattern of progression that must come to pass. We are playing a part in the whole. Every being knows its place. Every so often comes the cycle breaker, a person and a group they have always come to reset back to purity, giving back to nature. Because it has to come from the people, you have the voice and the choice.

"Your world is coming to a time of the cycle break. It is marked by a change in the ecosystem, sometimes great, sometimes subtle. Yours will be an uprising of the 'voice'. It is a time for the truth to rise from the depths of the belly of the Earth."

I turned the turkey feather over in my hand, wondering how it all fit together.

"You must find your voices.
You must find the voice of the Earth through you.
The birds are the sacred messengers of the heavens.
They can move through the Earth and sky realms. The

*turkey brings a strong connection to spirit, one that
will stay with you and guide you through finding your
voice and being that mouthpiece for the Earth."*

Back on this Earth plane I continued my hike to the
abandoned perlite cave close to the spot where the Apaches
had jumped to sacrifice themselves. On the way up I found
the second turkey feather. Of course it was a vision, standing
proudly upright on a small pile of freshly dug soil. It was a
marker for the grave of a small animal. My Apache guide
joined me, standing by my side, and he said:

*"You must always honour the transitions, no matter
how big or small. Each part of creation is sacred,
and it is the transition to death that offers the most
growth. It is the journey, not the destination."*

I had reached the perlite caves and they were full of Obsidian
tears scattered over the ground and hidden in the rocks. I
felt I was standing on the tears of many. Perlite is a type of
volcanic glass that gets saturated with water over a long
period of time. It's flaky and easy to dig into and holds an
extremely feminine energy that felt perfect to surround
these pockets of Obsidian's grandfather energy, and it was
the perfect balance. It was a really special experience to
collect these Apache Tears myself by hand from the perlite
in the land they were created in. When we got to the cave
there were a few people there, and by the sunset we were

on our own. I spent time asking for permission before I used my hand pick. I wondered where I would find the third feather, and just as I thought it, I found it, tucked lovingly behind my ear. It had been hidden there in plain sight. I loved it because it's something I often do when I find a feather: I pop it in my hair. I couldn't work out when it was placed there or if it just appeared. Neither mattered. I wondered what the last lesson or message they wished to offer me was and I heard a whisper in the wind that just simply said:

"You are the lesson, you are the gift."

All of nature offers us the opportunity to "feel" the memories of the past, present and future.

While digging in the perlite mine I was on the lookout for the special piece that would guide the rest of my connection to their ancestral guardians. I knew it was coming. I had been shown it, so I waited patiently. It found me through my partner Caitlin, who came to join me and dig next to me. She instantly found the biggest Apache Tear I've seen. We were like two kids at Christmas: it was the most exciting thing! She carefully dug it out, because they are fragile and break easily, and handed it to me saying, "This is for you."

Digging with care for obsidian in the pearlite cave.

At the time I was creating a crystal womb course – something that focused on healing the womb of ancestral pain and sexual trauma, with the assistance of crystals – and this stone stepped forward for some potent womb healing. Its energy jumped into my wombspace, spinning and cracking open, where its black light ran like water through me. Obsidian offers potent womb healing, because of how it connects to the ancestral line within us. It will sit and take you into the shadows your womb holds and helps ease the grip of fear and pain that can be held there.

 ## Apache Tears' Medicine

Over the past few months I have been deeply grateful for Apache Tears' black light. It found me as I was grieving, and as an emotional soother it does not stifle tears, but encourages us to cry, to feel it all, leaning into the uncomfortable. It's validating and comforting, supporting us in transmuting raw emotions into compassion and wisdom, showing us the time we need to heal or adjust to life-shattering truths, and this new reality we are in.

It knows the importance of the release and processing of negative emotions thoroughly when certain feelings threaten to sweep us away. Its energy is comforting and validating, showing you the breadth of your new emotional landscape. When you work with its black glow it engulfs your being, and can open the well of ancestors' grief within us. This is strangely comforting: grief can feel lonely, hard and long, and feeling your ancestors close through this stone helps us feel supported. Apache Tears hold, transmute and flow with you through your tears. For those of us who have buried grief through shame or are struggling to understand the negative emotions, it carefully unpicks these through the emotional layer of your body to bring understanding and a safe space to talk about our hardest memories and feelings. It's a good stone for therapy or to offer to anyone who is going through a hard emotional transition.

While I was digging for Apache Tears I felt that I was collecting pieces of myself hidden tears in layers of time. Whenever I uncovered one, I felt a rush of joy, a release from the Earth and from my heart.

"Pain is there because love is there. Don't sweep it away so soon because this offers a disservice to the love. Take all the time you need to heal."

Apache Tears

While working with Apache Tears Obsidian, the well within us bubbles up and overflows, and we can find that space to acknowledge collective grief to heal through the field. It also helps you forgive while releasing self-limiting beliefs. It's a good friend and will reset the emotional equilibrium in your body, and also has a knack for quieting the inner critic within you, when that harsh voice is telling you how you should feel and be. It has the extraordinary capacity to hold emotions with no judgement. It holds its own space strongly too, knowing emotional boundaries are needed, and does not need to be cleansed or charged. Think of this stone as your companion through hardship. Its goal is to help you accept your new reality and find your way back to your heart where peace lives. Let Apache

Apache Tears Obsidian.

Tears' energy surround and hold you now, as a black glow fills your field with a lightness and gentleness you did not expect.

A few months after writing this chapter something very magical happened and recalling the memory of it brings me to soft tears. I visited the Avebury stones in a very spontaneous trip, but that morning we just could not get out of the house and things took longer than necessary. Divine timing: I was exactly where I needed to be for a perfectly orchestrated moment. When indeed we did get there much later than planned, we were walking toward the beech tree portal at the Avebury site, passing the inner moon temple with its two great standing megaliths, and my feet led us there instead.

The inner moon temple is a place where I have seen many frequencies and higher rays moving often and as I approached

I greeted the megaliths. The stones were busy with a small group of people chatting happily, and two figures had placed hands on the left stone and were chanting beautifully. I stopped to close my eyes and listen. The woman was gently shaking a rattle and the older barefoot gentleman was saying a prayer in another language.

While I had the opportunity, I looked at the man closely. I noted he had Beech seed pods and a feather tied into his long hair. I smiled to myself: it took me back to my time in Superior, Arizona with my Native American guide, with the turkey feather in his hair and the pods I offered him. I believed the two had come on a pilgrimage to be here. I was entranced by the man and recognized his energy and chants of love for the Earth. I continued to stand silently listening while I heard the small group of people ask these travellers if they would like to take part in their peace circle, and they invited me too. I was standing next to the man, and I could just feel his energy radiating so much happiness, and I felt such joy.

I felt that my Native American guide's spirit lives on through this man and his kind eyes that looked directly into my soul. I marvelled at how magical spirit is, as the lady leading the circle said a beautiful passage she had written about Artemis the moon goddess. Then another gentleman suggested we create an energy ball between us and pass it around. The man had his turn to hold and add to this ball, which was growing fast, and watching him, I felt all the light frequency burst from my heart and angelic languages exploded from me as he handed it to me, pure joy and recognition of the intricate energies weaving in this moment. He held my gaze and I travelled into his heart.

I saw the moon, the bear and the fish, his guides and energies of the Earth and tribe. I felt an incredible amount of love for him. I recognized the divine father in him, this stranger who I had not spoken to aloud. We spoke the language of the heart. My light language was pure joy and up shifted the energy of the group who were all beaming. I giggled as we offered this love to the Earth, a beautiful moment with strangers who I believe gather at the moon gate every Sunday to send healing to the Earth.

I always find I meet the most incredible people at stone circles. Like guideposts, they bring us together to share stories

Earth healing with new friends in Avebury Moon Gate. To my left, hidden behind me, is the kind man with beech pods and feathers tied in his hair, whose energies connected me back to my ancestors.

and laughter. On leaving I approached the man: we silently locked eyes and hugged each other, no words needed – a long nurturing hug of appreciation for the moment, a slight bow of the head to each other and a smile. And off we went, never to see each other again unless while dreamwalking or journeying.

Sometimes it is the small moments that are the big moments. I believe this exchange, this moment with this ancestor at the stones, remains in my heart, and he will be there to meet me when I cross, in some way, shape or form. Maybe he will take on the shape of the great bear or the trout. I am so grateful to have this opportunity to write it and connect in this way.

Spontaneous Earth healing at Avebury Stones.

"Pain is there because love is there.
Don't sweep it away so soon because
this offers a disservice to the love.
Take all the time you need to heal."

Obsidian

Collected beech seed pod offerings, ready to fill with love
and intent, like seeds of light to offer back to the Earth.

Beech Pod

If you have sat in ceremony with me I will often bring a Beech Pod in. I carry them in my medicine bag and my heart does somersaults every time I find an empty seed pod on the forest floor.

The beech tree is the queen of the forest. Alongside her king, the oak, she upholds the faery way, the passageways into the Earth, sending the messages through her roots where they are carried by the winds into the roots and systems of all around her. Beech is known to offer protection and nourishment because she fans her branches out into a broad canopy that is useful for shelter. People once relied upon her beech nuts to keep themselves from starvation, and collecting them helped strengthen the bonds between the community or clans. If you are looking for wishes to be granted, cast your hopes and dreams into the Beech Pod and scatter them onto the Earth in thanks.

I was once driving through a tunnel of beech trees that arched over me and connected. I sent them so much love and appreciation in a great wave of light. They said, "We know you love us, thank you." They communicated that when we connect with one tree in love, they all feel it, even if that tree is on the other side of the world. Isn't that a magical thing to ponder on?

Beech Pod Ritual

Beech tree's energy helps you get closer to your ancestors, and their knowledge passed down through time and the stories that are stored deep within.

* Next time you are in the woods or forest look for some empty seed pods, and when you find some, ask the beech tree for permission to collect them.
* Hold them to your heart and make a wish, focusing your intent on what you heart wants to create. See that vision forming in your heart and bring all your senses to it to feel it through your whole body. Take some time on this and some full-bodied breaths.
* Hold the Beech Pod to your lips and blow your wishes, prayers and vision, wrapped in golden light, into its centre, and there imagine it glowing golden like a seed of light.
* Find somewhere to offer your wishes and prayers into the Earth by laying down the Beech Pod. I always offer it back to the beech tree in the folds of her roots. As you place it on the Earth, the faery guardians of spirit and place carry your love and light down into the Earth.
* Say a simple prayer to the Earth as you send the pod down to the Earth through the roots of the beech. Imagine its light taking root through the soil. There are many elemental friends watching over you, ready to help this wish bloom, and give thanks.

Offering love and wishes to the waters with Beech Pods. This was a womb healing session at St Mary's Well in Northumberland. The flowers offered represent the womb.

"Make a wish, focus your intent now on what you heart wants to create, plant it in light in the Beech Pod and say a simple prayer to the Earth as you send it down to the Earth through the roots of the beech. There are many elemental friends watching over you, ready to help this wish bloom."

Beech Pod

Crystal grid created on Alnmouth Beach,
Northumberland, with Sea Coal, goldenrod, sea bindweed,
yarrow and shells, all growing or found on the coastline.

Sea Coal

As I was walking along the coast of Northumberland, I noticed the vast amount of Sea Coal scattered across the sand. I picked up four small, water-washed pieces that sparkled "hello" at me as the sun caught their textured edges.

They have a soft feel, a shining surface and are as light as a feather. They sparked mystery and intrigue. Never have I looked at coal in this way: it felt like I had uncovered something hidden that had always been in plain sight. I loved the merging of water and fire within the stones in my hand, and the feel of the sea on them and the fire within them. I felt I was holding unified stones that challenge us to make changes that enable growth.

My father is local to the area and told me that people used to come down to the beach to collect them for their hearths when money was tight, and there was a "Sea Coaler" community in a nearby beach that collected the coals that washed up on the beach by horse and cart. There are even stories of Sea Coal being carried by fishermen on their boats for good fortune. It was nice to connect with the hands of those who also found this Coal as treasure to them, which sustained them and kept their hearts and hearths warm through the cold winter months.

Coal is a sedimentary rock, formed of the remains of dead plant matter such as ferns that died in swamp lands. Over millions of years these plants were buried under rocks, and after heat and pressure moulded them, very little remained apart from carbon, where they became coal. They hold in their energy field the energetic power of that time of Earth. So who better to understand the Earth's inner order than the energy of the ancient plant matter and soil? Coal is mostly made of carbon, which is abundant on Earth. It is mostly found in rocks, the ocean, atmosphere and in living organisms, including us, although we are moving from a carbon-based template to silica, crystalline template. Coal is also a source that's found in huge deposits in my grandmother's ancestral home of the Khasi hills in Meghalaya, where the territory has rich deposits of sub-bituminous coal, belonging to the Eocene age (36–56 million years ago). My ancestors' energy is woven through these pages, over-lighting them with love.

Coal encourages us to look at the flow state and intelligence of Earth, and how she takes care of herself, trusting her cycles and moving unquestionably with her rhythms. It offers us the opportunity to tune in to our very own flow state, to be totally grounded in being here, now. I paused on the beach to sit on the rocks and hold these lumps of bituminous coal. They did feel as if they were weighing me down and balancing the air within my systems with the Earth. They offered me the visual of one of those swinging Newton's Cradle ball sets that many people had on their desks in the 1990s.

I have been sitting with the impact of coal on our environment: I know it's a controversial one considering the issues of renewable resources. But coal is one of the most ancient energy resources our Earth holds, and speaks to us of the Earth's progress. It is ironic that a stone, when burnt, is destructive to the planet, but its essence speaks about biodiversity and supporting life on Earth from the micro-organisms, plants, animals and humans. Coal is a very complex and intelligent energy. It speaks to the Earth's gravitational pull and spin, and the biodiversity of its core. It's so keen to show us the mysterious deep biosphere of life within the Earth. It shows these underground ecosystems in pockets of extreme heat, which are home to so much undiscovered life that has been there since the birth of Earth.

"Cause and effect play an important part in the universe. Imagine you are that silver ball, swinging on the outside; you can choose to radiate so much light, and that light hits beings and spectrums on the farthest side of the universe that will feel a ripple effect. You must keep the momentum going. Increase the light and get others to amplify this light with you. The momentum can carry fast especially when it is of high positive intent, but you have to start the light's movement. When you make a choice to carry the momentum of light in your cells it activates others you come into contact with through their hearts. Soon all of the silver balls on Newton's cradle are moving in union, and you are not recognizable from the thousands that join you: you are one force, a comet of light and heat that supports the planet."

Sea Coal

That day on the beach, it was a welcome reminder from coal of our force in numbers, which has the potential to flick the change switch. For a while I enjoyed watching my son play in the rock pools, and the Coal enabled a sense of rest and peace deep within my muscles for a while. One thing is sure: coal understands the mechanics of this Earth, even if I don't. It understands the process of this planet's evolution and heat distribution, and showed me thermal bio-chambers of heat locked in the Earth that allow life to flourish. Coal is very illusive around dark matter, seeming to understand it and know it well. Not being a scientist or educated in any way around any of this, this information eludes me and makes me feel totally out of my depth. Coal makes me feel like I'm back at school, studying a subject I am not entirely sure I even want to take. With the right mind to process, this ally can be illuminating to bring forward knowledge on permaculture and the ways we can work with solar energy. As such it is a teacher stone; it understands the balance of work and play, when to take action and when to rest.

Coal asks us to look at our environment, and ask yourself how environmental frequencies are affecting you and your energy field in a positive and negative light. It draws our awareness to electro-motive forces in and around the Earth and the need to cleanse and clear the feet chakras often. Placing coal at your feet will assist with this. There are many types of coal, from this Sea Coal to jet, which is a precursor to coal, and on a microscopic level it resembles the structure of wood, helping you dig through your family tree to release past patterns and held trauma particularly in the lungs and heart. Jet speaks to the druid, the tree keeper and the roots of the Earth, conjuring visions of the

Imbuing the energies of warmth and opening
within the body and chakra column.

tree of life, and the union of the Earth and sky that is felt within us, with Jet acting as an anchor to heaven and Earth within our core, supporting that flow and understanding deep in our bones.

Anthracite

The hardest form and higher quality of coal is called Anthracite. It has higher concentrations of carbon and graphite with a silver or bronze glow. It is a diffusing energy. It breaks things down, whether it's matter, emotions or thoughts. It's very effective on the mental field, creating pockets of space in the mental field, helping you to release the inner fog and mental static around you, so your mind and nervous system can relax more deeply. Its energy is more electric and sweeps through the lightbody, confronting stagnant and heavy density, standing its ground and surrounding this inner smog in its frequency until it dissolves,

Gridding on the coast of Northumberland with foraged Sea Coal that is scattered across the beach.

lifting the space within you. It is truly expansive and can stretch and move to surround vast layers of unresolved trauma in the Earth grids and on land to dissipate it. Its energy likes to burrow down deep within to find pulses of energy that need to be reconnected within you, and it also does this within the Earth, reconnecting pathways. I love how it helps us recognize the beauty in all things, and the balance within the ecosystems, like Sea Coal's message to us. We need to get into the space of appreciating the subtle balance of all things, the times life can be so wonderful and so hard at the same time, and how we can see the beauty around us but also feel the pain. Anthracite found me in this reflective mood, where I was dipping into lower mood states, and it lifted me from anxiety. It has a lifting action in its energetic pull, helping soothe depression, worried thoughts and anxiety as it calms the nerves and protects from panic attacks. A nice trick if you have a tumbled piece is to rub it or place it on your temples or third eye if you have a headache.

Sea Coal Exercise

I asked the Sea Coal that I have collected the best ways we could work together, and it gave me the visual of a pocket of warmth within my body that I could tune in to and bring my body security and safety. It is important that we feel secure and safe: I witness people during sessions who have so much built-up worry, anxiety and trauma that they need to disassociate, so their energy literally jumps out of their body. Sea Coal wants to help us find the warm places of our body so we can self-soothe through hard times.

For this vision you are going to be gazing at the photograph of the Sea Coal crystal grid to tune in. Ask in your mind for it to show you where you need to bring warmth and healing light to your body. Focus your gaze on the central coal stone until, in your mind's eye, you see it set alight in a golden orange flame. When you see it activating through connection and intent you welcome this flame into your body.

★ Breathe it in, feeling and visualizing its orange flame entering your body.

★ Follow the stream of its energy into your body, observing, not attaching, being curious as to where it goes.

★ You watch is settle in your body, and take note of where it is, as this is the space where you need most warmth.

★ Watch as it nestles into the spot, creating a small orange fire that radiates warmth around your organs, tissues, muscles, cells, membranes, bones and waters.

★ Allow the fire to expand and grow with each inhale: all you need to do is focus on the fire and the warmth as it begins to grow through you.

★ You observe it grow and touch all parts of you as it expands to fill you.

★ While holding that visual of golden orange flames rippling through all of you, you affirm out loud: "I AM safe, I AM secure, I feel the warmth of love."

★ Take a moment to wrap both arms around your body, and give yourself a hug.

★ Give your body a moment of gratitude. Your body is a beautiful temple that holds your soul; it deserves your love.

"Life can flourish in the hardest, most extreme environments, and if it can flourish there, you can flourish here."

Sea Coal

Close-up of Scolecite.

Scolecite

I have this innate trust that the universe brings
us the tools we need to heal. It communicates
through stones and crystals, as it does with trees,
animals and flowers. Always take a sacred moment
with a crystal gift that someone gives to you: it
is a sacred message from the Earth. The angels,
guides and helpers have moved their energies
through this gift giver to get this energy to you.

Scolecite is a member of the zeolite family, a secondary crystal
that forms in cavities of granite, basalt and syenites. It occurs
in a range of colours from white to pink, purple, yellow and
colourless. In the crystal grid on page 109 we connect with
the energies of a white Scolecite from India. First reported to
Western science in 1813 in Germany, it was named for the Greek
word *"skōlēx"*, meaning "worm". Some people say that this is
because when Scolecite is heated with a blow torch, it curls up.
If you look deeper to the spiritual meaning of the worm, it is one
of rebirth and regeneration, which holds true to the energetic
messages Scolecite offers.

I have always admired Scolecite's need to support and hold
the bones of us, our foundations, working with the crown to

bring stability and comfort and equally mirroring that to the root chakra, the two chakra entry points to the physical layer of the body. It understands the delicate need for balance and structure and for crown and root to hold the body through change. I have had lots of Scolecite from India over time, and its feminine white aesthetic and the way the light glows from its facets in raw form has always captivated me and danced in my heart. When found raw, Scolecite forms these beautiful fan shapes. It looks and can be so delicate, but when layered together these are strong, reminding us that no matter how delicate we feel we have such a strength within us to weather any storm. I witnessed my Scolecite crystal activating with the energies of the portal and aligning with them. When it fully attuned it asked to be placed on my third eye. Here it brought a high current of energy into my eyes, and its high vibrational light flickered to the back of the corneas, scanning them, opening, unlocking and unpicking.

This crystal works by moving its pure white, cooling energy through your bones to strengthen them. With a slight feeling of air, it cleanses and nudges any disharmony it finds within your energetic pathways to move it on. Often it is the crown that receives its cool rays first as there it opens it as much as it can to support higher-vibrational soul-fragment energy to integrate from the soul star chakra.

It often shows me the images of blocked pathways in the body, and once cleared it sends in a Quartz crystal circuit board to drop in and reconnect you to your divine blueprint. It works with crystalline templates and pieces, as if bandaging up holes and cracks within the lightbody. As it drops them in,

Crystal grid of scolecite, quartz and chrysoprase to bring activation and cleansing to the body and throat.

they send out a ripple of harmony through the field, letting all those around you know that you are vibrating high. It wishes to serve you by bringing you to optimum energetic health, which I know is no mean feat, but the more you work with it, the faster its flow moves through you. Once it's scanned your systems and understands them, it moves faster. There is something very intelligent about the way it works and interacts with the body: it's like a technician, tinkering away. It isn't one for talking too much, and is about action.

Scolecite is of a very high angelic connection, and its way of cleansing, purifying and detoxifying the mind, body and spirit is invaluable at this time of rapid change on the Earth. It will expand the crown chakra and open a funnel of light to fully connect and integrate energies from your higher chakras. It connects intimately with the crown, skull, brain, eyes, ears, jaw and throat. If you have even had an Indian head massage or cranio-sacral therapy, and experienced that feeling of someone holding your crown, close your eyes and call back that feeling: this is the feeling Scolecite offers you. Holding hands through times of energetic change. The guardians of Scolecite are the white-winged ones: the high-vibrational pure beings, the angels, the pure white birds, the swans and snow owls. Connecting with the messages of the air elements, it takes you up higher to explore cosmically, to be able to communicate with entities and pure ones of other dimensions and worlds. It is a valuable tool to work with the ancient star energies our ancestors listened too, and interplanetary contact and lessons various cultures have learned over the Earth's ages.

Journey to Meet Scolecite's Medicine

Scolecite invites you to journey up and out with it through your crown chakra.

* Take a few moments to align with your heart through your breath, and to hold the intention for only the highest and greatest healing light to pass through your lightbody and all aspects and versions of you. Call in the protective light of the angels of purity and grace.
* Connect with the photograph on page 109 and when you feel you have interlinked, woven with it and received its light with your breaths, allow a Scolecite portal to form around your crown.
* It magnetizes you it with its light.
* As you begin to pass through it, feel it scanning and connecting with your energy, templates and lightbody. It is giving you a full-body scan. You may feel places its light is pulsing and moving within you; allow for that feeling and breathe it in with acceptance.
* Take your time on that step, as long as you need, noting where it's travelling to and what it wishes to show you.
* Scolecite's high vibration raises the frequencies around and within you now, bringing the angels in around you.
* You feel them drop in now and they form a circle around you and surround you in a sphere of white and golden healing light.
* Breathe in this light and feel your cells breathing it in, your organs and tissue, muscle and membranes breathing it in.

* Taking your time to be with this fully with your breath.
* Scolecite drops in crystals circuits into your lightbody to fill the spaces it is working on with you. They upgrade, and replace old and heavy density in your body now.
* Be in this healing sphere for as long as you need, receiving light and love from the angels of purity and Scolecite.
* When you feel refreshed and recalibrated, call your energy back down through this portal space and into your heart, closing any portals around you with the intent. You see the Scolecite portal above your crown dissolve in light; it is closed.

Sealing and binding the crystals grid with quartz.

"We cannot unsee what we have witnessed over time, but we can heal the wounds of the eyes that are closed to truth.

We can re-frame, heal and access the past where we have witnessed pain, fear, slavery and persecution, but without going to the root core of where it is held in the body we are not allowing ourselves to open fully. There are many layers to healing as you know, and what the mind offers as solutions to trauma, sometimes the body does not want. Be open to what works for you and build resonance with the healing practices that your body responds to. Do not overlook your foundations: your inner structures, the bones. My light supports the bones of you, the structure and more often than not the release of outdated structures you have created around you."

Scolecite

Taking my Carnelian out to grid in Oregon, US.

Carnelian

When I was living in Virginia, USA, I received a message from someone online who had been guided to me. This often happens to me, as the right stones and people find me at the right time.

This person said "I love rocks and minerals, and have collected crystals with my family from our land in Washington state since I was a child. I have a small collection of Carnelian stones and Agates that I think are for you."

We got talking and struck up a friendship, and of course she lived close to me in Washington, DC. I remember walking to her home to meet her one day. I had a little woven basket with me, full of chimes that jingled sweetly with every step I took. When I knocked at her door I was greeted by this cool 1970s-looking tarot reader, and we instantly connected over the stones and our love of the esoteric. I loved that she had enjoyed sharing this hobby with her family, which reminded me of crystal hunting with my son. In Virginia, where we lived at the time, we had some land containing what felt like endless woods, which was also a hub of star being frequencies anchoring. We found a vein of cloudy quartz and so much golden mica, which we had fun collecting together.

She was a collector too, and by that time my brand &Crystals was going from strength to strength, selling small pockets of curated crystals: special pieces that almost always found me. She gifted me this piece of Carnelian she had collected with a naturally formed heart in the centre. She felt this last collection she found was very special and wanted to see what I thought. We spoke of the way she found them. She was walking through the woodland and her attention was called over to one patch of Earth with a natural rock formation that looked like a woman's yoni with legs open, and in the centre of this space were the Carnelian pieces on the surface of the Earth, and no digging was needed to collect them. She took only what felt right and when she got them home to wash them gently she noticed every one of them had a yoni marking on them. As we spoke she showed me a photo of the land and the stones that guarded them, and I saw Mary Magdalene standing there, over lighting this find of womb healing stones.

I of course gratefully took them and sat them out on my land to connect with the Earth there. I witnessed the stones sending golden threads of light out to all the trees around my home, connecting deeply with them all. When you hold these raw untouched pieces up to the light their banded layers of agate shone through. I never sold these pieces: I felt they must be given as a gift, because when crystals are given as a gift by protectors there's a very deep honouring of the Earth involved and the Earth greatly appreciates it. I work with these meaningful pieces with some of my clients and many have found their way to shamanic womb healers and fertility specialists across the globe.

Carnelian is a stone of the goddess, and when working with her the spirit of the goddess comes through: the unified balance of the maiden, mother and crone. I have often found when I worked with Carnelian the three goddesses appear to me: Mary Magdalene (maiden) is a strong over-lighting guide to steer us back to our womb hearts. Goddess Isis comes in as a guardian holding the keys of the divine mother, and the Celtic goddess Ceridwen comes as the crone. Hers is the cauldron of wisdom she stirs within our wombs and hearts and she often comes to circle stirring a Carnelian cauldron. The Egyptians called Carnelian the fertile menstrual blood of the mother goddess, Isis. Carnelian carries the stories and records of our planet, stabilizing and anchoring us

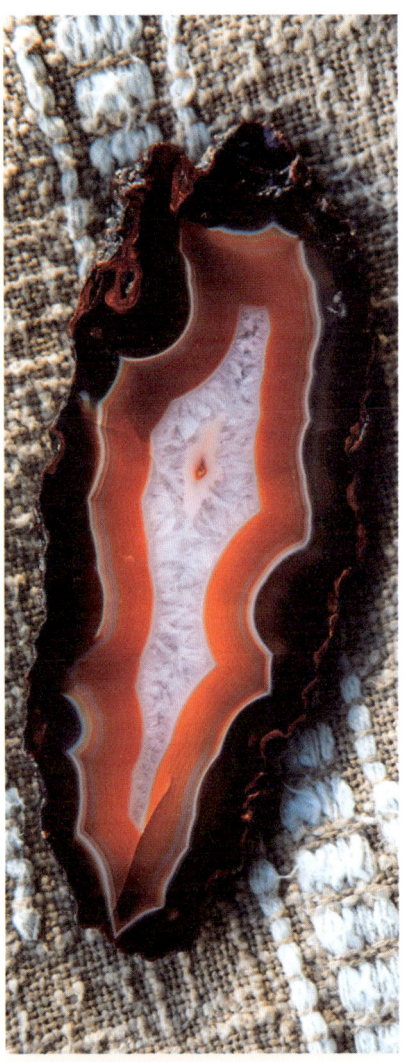

My piece of Carnelian that has assisted in a lot of womb healing.

into the present. Its warmth is not only felt in the womb but in the throat too where she brings forward your voice, supporting you to reclaim your songs. We know that the womb and throat are closely interwoven, and Carnelian is sometimes called a singer's stone.

A Carnelian gift is one of love, warmth, passion and uniting sovereign power within you, and the fire she brings to your sacred chakra and womb is not overpowering, but is a gentle flame stirring passion, sexuality and your divine feminine to stand tall. She also boosts the flow of energy through the body and picks you up when you are low. Her energy is all wise woman who knows who she is, and knows with faith what she is here to offer, and these qualities she imbues within you. As you can sense, Carnelian is an incredible sexual healer: the darker shades bring a masculine energy in balance and heal traumas to the sexual organs in the reproductive systems of both sexes, from this life and past lives. The lighter shades with the golden tones bring a reminder of the lightness of life, a golden ray that lifts us emotionally when facing this deep work. It is full of life-force energy and will boost yours! It also stimulates the blood flow and energy flow through the whole body.

Offer Carnelian love and she will return the love tenfold. Her energy encourages love between parent and child, stimulating our heart to appreciate the beauty and gifts those around offer us, especially the Earth. It brings acceptance of the cycles of life. I often have it in my medicine bag when working with those transitioning their bodies, as it works to ease the fear of death, protecting them and guiding the soul in its next onward journey, and it pairs so beautifully with rose quartz in this loving intent.

Crystal Meditation to Connect With Your Womb Heart

Connecting with the activating fire within your heart will help you transmute and activate your womb, to bring warmth and love to your wombspace and your sacral chakra.

This is important because it brings healing, empowerment and passion. It brings the awareness of your sexuality and the safety of knowing that you are the creator of your journey, and that you are in control of your own destiny.

You will need Carnelian – to place on your sacral chakra, the centre of the womb, and rose quartz – to place on your heart.

★ Seated, take three deep grounding breaths into your heart. Each breath is pure white light, which moves through you, opening your heart. You start to see or imagine your heart's light beaming out of you in all directions. Speak this aloud:
    I AM OPEN
    I AM HELD
    I AM GROUNDED.
★ Imagine a bolt of pure white light descending from the heavens, moving down right through your higher chakras and filling your crown up. It opens and expands it as it moves down through you into your third eye, then your throat, opening and expanding them in light. Finally it moves into your solar plexus and sacral chakra where it settles.

* You can see this beam of light moving down through you. It has opened all of your chakras in a brilliant white light.
* Once you have done this lie down and lay the rose quartz on your heart and the Carnelian at your womb.
* Feel their weight and accept their energies into your body. The rose quartz brings a pink glow all the way through your body, allowing it to move through into the places it needs to go. Observe its trail of light.
* You bring your awareness to the Carnelian crystal on your womb. Again you follow the glowing orange energy of the stone as it enters your womb. Be aware of where it goes. As it moves through your womb it lights it up; it ignites a gentle fire within you. Flicking golden and orange flames warm up your wombspace. Those flames start to expand through your womb and outside of it. They hold you in a golden bubble of light. I want you to breathe in on this visual and feel the warmth these rays bring you.
* Bring your awareness to your heart. We are going to create a beautiful arc of pink light that comes up from your heart and moves down toward your womb. It plugs into your womb as we connect heart to womb in light. As it connects it sends through a beautiful wave of pink love.
* Know that you are loved in all you do: you are accepted, worthy and appreciated.
* Take time to sit in these pink and golden rays as they work through all layers of you, through all cells structures and timelines to bring change, to bring love and to move such a depth and breadth of light through you.

"I am not scared of the dark spaces,

The damp, the cold and unloved.

I remain a detached and neutral friend.

For many of you these spaces
feel scary or comfortable,

They challenge you when you're
too tired to face them.

When that is the case seek help,

And I am here to stoke your inner
fire, to fan the flames within.

I rise to the challenge of change,
of freedom and service,

Fostering self-confidence and passion.

Wild and wise, and so we rise."

Carnelian

Grounding crystal grid to access hidden wisdom
and connect with the ancestors. Created with
raw Flint from the USA, staurolite from the USA,
Flint from Avebury and beech pods collected at
the beech trees in Glastonbury Chalice Well.

Flint

Flint is a common mineral, a type of quartz rock that forms naturally within chalk and limestone and is found all over the world. It's one of my favourite shamanic stones to bring into ceremony and one you can ask the Earth for while out walking.

It's really an exceptional grounding stone, emitting Earth's purest vibrations with a raw and powerful energy and helping us individually on our quest for self-discovery. It helps you to peel back the layers to see who you once were. This is an invaluable stone for past life healing.

Flint was one of the most powerful stones to guide me at the beginning of my journey. Back when I was a footwear designer, I was working in Milan and hadn't fully immersed myself in the crystal kingdoms. I found myself in a dusty little crystal store down a little back street, where I saw two pieces of brown Flint. There was nothing special about them, just two big brown lumps of rock. But when I held them I heard warriors' calls and the beat of a drum. The connection was made. I was taken to a Navajo settlement and felt this stone connect me with something deep within myself; it connected me to my masculine voice. The sounds and visions became so overwhelming that I had to leave the store, but not without buying those pieces of Flint first. When I got home I put those stones away, knowing that they were not for now. They intimidated me: such a big Earth call rippled through them.

I'm not sure how much time passed before I decided to get them out and sat in a circle of crystals that I had constructed. Sitting in a circle of crystals is what we used to do in Atlantis, and is one of the most beautiful and powerful things you can do. I decided to hold one of the pieces in my hand and instantly it took me into a shamanic trance. I was pulled into the stone, into the Earth and my body started to rock back and forth uncontrollably. I was tested with the wish to surrender but I was scared; it felt like this Earth energy was taking over me. But it felt familiar, like I had done this many times before, so I trusted it.

Flint took me with ease to some of my past lives as a Native American. In one I was a medicine man in a hut. I sat around a small fire, smoke filled the air and it was night time because the only light was the soft golden glow of the fire that flickered across my features. I heard an eagle call and instantly became the eagle, sharing its consciousness, seeing through its eyes, observing from above. I realized that I was moving my consciousness and energy with the fire and smoke, up through the opening at the top of the hut to connect and be with the bird. It was my first recollection of shapeshifting: I was in two places at once, and in a quantum realizing that I'm in all, and in many places at once.

Flint spoke to me in a sombre, serious tone, with a strong masculine voice that was very direct and forthright, he said that

I had two paths in front of me. One was to walk through the fire, to work with the land and to unlock ancient keys of druid wisdom with the trees, original Earth and golden age blueprints. His voice seemed urgent. I felt the pull of him directing me this way. The other path was with the stones, where I would teach and guide. It would be much gentler and angelic, and each would get me to where I needed to go. Of course, I took the crystals route and it was not long after that moment that my company &Crystals was born. But really both paths were and are the same, as I'm doing elements of both. Flint has been with me from the start as an initiator stone.

My favourite pieces of Flint have been collected from sacred sites. I like the blue-black tones of the Flint from Avebury, which is scattered over the fields on the way up to West Kennet Long Barrow. It was a piece that I collected recently that spoke through my *Songs of the Stones Oracle* deck (it is in the flint photographed on page 122). Holding it, it showed me the footprints of the ancestors walking the soil of Avebury, on their pilgrim route to the stones. It was insistent that we see how our ancestors' sacrifice created the foundations for us and where we are now. Just as we will continue to live, love and sacrifice for the future children and their children.

Flint asks you:

"What are you ready to sacrifice to move forward?

"Sometimes an offering of love is needed to give to the Earth, great spirit and the elementals to show your willingness and readiness."

Avebury Flint from West Kennet Long Barrow.

I had an experience of unknowingly sacrificing something at Avebury when there on a fertility pilgrimage with a friend. I had taken my little basket of stones, oils and instruments and with me, my favourite hand-carved pine wood sistrum, which made the most glorious twinkly song when rattled. The fae loved it, and I'd ring it every time I wandered through the forest or woods and they would follow me. I had it while walking the Long Barrow then on the way back down I realized it was not in my basket. I can't express how much this was my favourite instrument. I took it everywhere and it was nowhere to be seen. After a lot of dramatic sighs, my friend said, "It was an offering to the ancestors," to which I asked why it had to be such a precious and important thing to me, and she said that sometimes big wishes needed big offerings.

Connect With Flint's Medicine

If you are ready to move forward and need a strong Earth voice, consider working with Flint. You can gather some when in nature and construct a circle for yourself to sit in. Eight to ten pieces will suffice. Take time to call their energy in and collect them in an intentful way. Ask the Earth for them, and ask permission to take them home, knowing that you can always give them back after you are done. Take time to connect with them, wash them in warm water and explore their texture, angles and curves, knowing you chose the bits that want to work with you and are ready to do so.

It is helpful to create a ceremony and ritual around this, as it is a special connection you are fostering with the Earth.

* Turn down the lights, light some candles, burn some sacred smoke to cleanse yourself and your space and take some deep breaths to connect with the Earth.

* Gather your stones together and ask them to work with you to help you connect and remember. Then take some time to create a circle big enough for you to sit in the centre. You in effect are gridding yourself: you become the central crystal in the grid.

* Connect with each piece of Flint in turn by looking at them and acknowledging them, envisioning their energy glowing on connection ready to work with you.

* Close your eyes and begin to breathe into your root, your lower spine, being very aware of the circle of energies around you. Begin to breathe them into your root.

* Filling your root with their brown energy until it is full, you might begin to feel slight pressure, feeling the flow from all the stones coming into your body, each breath magnetizing it deeper into your body, through all layers.

* When your root is full, pull this energy up into your sacral chakra. See and feel the continuous flow from the stones into your root and up.

* You continue to carry the energy up through your chakras. Once each is full, breathe deeper and bring it up to the next. To the solar plexus, then heart, throat and third eye, until finally you are in your crown and the energy has built up through your whole body. You feel so grounded: feel it gather and start to bring pressure to your crown ready to expand out of your crown. When you are ready, let this energy release like a waterfall of light all around you.

"Open your eyes to the cycles of rebirth that you and the Earth are moving through. You are resurrecting yourself over and over every day, in every moment with every breath. You are a whole new person each day. Don't cling too tightly to the past and move with the new energies around you.

Who do you want to be today?
What do you wish to feel? How do
you wish to make others feel?

Breathe with the Earth and bring your
heart into alignment with her.

Notice the many millions of footsteps scattered across her surface. Many have walked before you, and many will continue after you. You become part of the music score of this planetary song. Built on the bones, songs and stories of the ancestors that pepper the Earth and sweeten the soil.

Surrender to the never-ending spiral,
knowing that nothing is permanent,
everything is sacred and that you are
a walking miracle and a mystery.

Tend to the sacred in you.

Because there is no one, or nothing
more sacred than you."

Flint

Eudialyte, with light language to enhance its energies.

Eudialyte

I always feel the legends and stories around the stones. Even their names can offer us so much insight into their energies. If the ancestors took the time to carry their stories via oral tradition for so long, there is a beautiful underlying truth to them, no matter how much stories get embellished over time.

While writing this book I often wondered who or when the next ancestor will appear, and in Eudialyte it feels like a pivotal moment of remembrance of an old way, an old lesson or teaching. Eudialyte marks the passage of time with us, as the Earth is stepping into a new cycle. I am finding that each ancestor is finding me, and you, in perfect alignment with where we are and what we need at this moment on the journey. Of course, everything is perfect. Our journeys are all the same and shared. The stones are bringing us together to see this. Eudialyte is a complex silicate mineral, commonly found in granular patterns. It ranges in colour from pink to red, brown and violet, often having inclusions of black tourmaline. Western science first found it in Greenland, by F. Stromeyer in 1819, but it can also be found in Canada, Russia, Madagascar and the US.

Initiations of Eudialyte

When I first came across this stone, its red glow lit the space and it glowed with secrets and mystery until I picked it up and could not put it down. And when I forged that connection it glowed through my hands and moved straight to my heart. I couldn't put my finger on why I needed it so badly, but I did. It came home with me and asked to walk in my dream state with me. The only words it offered me were "Things aren't always what they seem."

As I closed my eyes with it on my heart, its energy emerged in a smoky haze as a peaceful Sámi guide, who gazed at me through the smoke of a small campfire. He had kind eyes that opened like windows offering a flow of Earth energy to connect with. His skin was waxy and worn, with a slight red glow to his cheeks that warmed his face. I couldn't move past his eyes; all connection flowed through them unlike any ancestor I have encountered yet. They drew me in, sparking aqua-blue light at me, and all I could feel was that these eyes had seen so many things. I could see through them as if they were mine, where they showed me his home, and land and a great many grand pine forests that seems to stretch endlessly to the sky. He smiled and held out his hand to me, which was full of pine needles that he lit. The pine tree seemed important to him and his culture. He wished to speak to me about this tree that held an important place in his healing. He took a seat in the snow and said:

"This tree watches the transitions of Earth from up high. It is home to the eagles and owls. I watch them come and go. Can you imagine its perspective up high, how small we are and how little we matter to the eagle? But here on the ground, we matter a great deal, and the Earth, she expects us to be the custodians of her energies, protecting, honouring and valuing. And up there in the sky there are the protectors of the winds who have their worlds and their place to protect. Each of us has a role, interlocking with the other, affecting the other so inconsequential individually, but on the whole we need each other to move forward. We are to see through the eyes of the eagle and the bark of the pine. We are to listen to the calls of the elk and the whispers of the winds.

"I am a mere shadow, a whisper of the past, and the past lessons of my tribe are being lost and erased, which is why I come back.

"I am everything and nothing, belonging everywhere and nowhere. My people have no fixed roots, which serves us in the lessons of attachment. I am happy to let go of a place, lovingly say goodbye then embrace the excitement for the next space I will find myself in, anticipating the animals and birds I will meet. We move with the reindeer and elk, we serve the animals and the land. How can I serve the land with you now? How can we be of service?

I took his hands in mine and asked for his wisdom, and told him that we are listening. My mind jumped to the stone Eudialyte and how it fits into this exchange, and he heard my thoughts. He said that sometimes things do go the way we expect them to, and we can start in one place and in moments move somewhere completely different, and that it's about being present and listening and open to quick change. He said:

> "This is what is coming at this point in Earth's history: quick change and fast movement. You all need to be ready to surrender and flow with this and not fight against it. There is a rumble in the forests and a quickening in the energies of the mountains, and the opening of light that's moving at a fast pace. If you are not open to receiving this it will pass you by and its momentum will be wasted."

I asked him to be more specific and we jumped into the Earth's records and saw that from the date 5 May 2025 a high percentage of light is moving into the Earth. The trees and stones are preparing to conduct higher percentage of unity consciousness, which will shake up the currents around us, and we need to flow and not fight.

He smiled at me and said:

> "See, we always come back to the place we needed to be, and all this talk of quick movement and momentum:

*Eudialyte holds this . . . it has the ability to hold,
guide and direct you through currents of change
and ground your heart when it can get too much."*

Not in any moment did my Sámi guide appear with this
stone in his hands. He only ever held the Earth and the pine,
and I suspect he has never held this stone, only known of its
majesty and connected with it in the Earth. He continued:

*"Why would I need to own this stone? It is the Earth's,
and it does what it needs to from within the Earth,
with no interference from me. And that is a lesson
humans must learn: to not interfere with nature.
It understands its place, we must understand ours."*

And so it was about the stone all along, but the stones are
just one piece, the trees and forests, the animals and birds
are another piece of us. We need to work with all of them,
and recognize them all as our friends and helpers.

I felt the loving connection to this ancestor radiating
through his sparkling eyes, and I felt inclined to ask him
a final question: "Can you show me something magical?"

He smiled and squeezed my hands, then let them go,
and conjured up a spirit drum to call in the ancient energies
of his people. The most beautiful sounds came from his
mouth. Suddenly there was a ring of fire around us, which
lit the shadows of the space golden. The drum started
to build the energy around us. It called energies up from

the Earth and they danced around us, taking part in this celebration. I could feel the movement around me as if we were being lifted up by the air. It must have been what levitating feels like. There were sparks of light dancing around me, and shimmering dust. My guide just smiled with his eyes closed, caught up in his trance, happily drumming, not for me or him, but for nature.

He made an animal call, and suddenly two large reindeer came in close through the trees. The most magical thing then happened: the reindeer bowed as if welcoming us onto their backs. I felt like I was in a fairy tale, where the most surreal things were happening that just seemed natural. Feelings of bliss and colours and sounds became hyper real. We got on the reindeer and took to the skies where I got to see the world below from the eyes of the winged ones. My bones were resonating with the stories of Santa Claus flying through the air with his reindeer; all I could feel was this jolly figure riding through the sky. I felt a strong connection to him through this tribe. We saw the Northern Lights light up the sky and a feel of reverence for all these things fell into my being. It truly was magical: the tall pines, the snow and the colours.

He said to me:

"There are not many places in this [solar] system where you can experience all of this at once. The colours of this world are majestic and ever changing. Always look for the beauty to inspire you."

Sámi Medicine

I have been speaking with Eudialyte since this exchange with this Sámi medicine man. It is truly a stone of transition, and what transition could be greater than the one we are living through on Earth at this time, moving ever faster to live in unconditional, loving 5D reality? It holds a slow and steady energy, which will help us accept change. It is an all-round emotional support system that brings a calm and stabilizing voice through emotional ups and downs, helping us to navigate feelings of bereavement and loss, abandonment and rejection. All of the core wounds that will continually surface through life, as part of this human existence, Eudialyte is part of. All we can do is remind ourselves daily that we are so loved, and we are here for a reason, even if that reason is just to be, to observe and to radiate love. This sums up Eudialyte's heart energy: slow, steady acceptance of change and love.

After having my own experience with this guide and this crystal I started to read more about the Sámi people. They are the indigenous people who inhabit Sápmi (their preferred name for Lapland) and surrounding arctic regions of Norway, Sweden, Finland and Russia's Kola Peninsula. They have lived in harmony with nature for thousands of years, making them one of Europe's oldest surviving cultures. A semi-nomadic tribe, they are known for their reindeer herding, mastery of survival and magical and colourful embroideries, clothing and artwork.

There is a story that connects them to the stone Eudialyte, which they called "Sámi Blood" in Sámi folklore. There was a battle between Swedish soldiers and the Sámi people. There was so much violence and death, the Sámi blood was spread across the tundra and legend says that their blood formed Eudialyte gemstones. Soldiers carried this stone as a protective talisman to ward off negative energy The spiritual leader, or shaman of the Sámi people is called a Nåjd in Swedish and Noaidi in Sámi. During ceremonies at poignant times, most notably winter solstice, the Noaidi would become the bridge between spirit and Earth by working with the plant medicine of the magic mushroom *Amanita muscaria*.

This mushroom would give the sensation of flying, and both the reindeer and shamans would eat this mushroom to give the sensation of flying. So you can see where the idea of a flying Santa Claus could be based on the story of the Sámi shaman flying with their plant ally. Santa Claus' origin is from the indigenous cultures of the north, including the Sámi peoples in Lapland. It is said that the shaman would visit a family to conduct a ceremony, eat the mushroom, beat his drum and start to chant, then they went into a trance and received visions. I experienced this very vividly with my Sámi guide (without the mushrooms, I have to add) but received the sensation of the intense colours and flight.

I was sad to find that in the 19th century the church targeted these Sámi shamans, accusing them of witchcraft. They burnt their drums and stopped their ceremonies. So many of their traditions disappeared. This story is as old as time: one of foreigners coming and taking the land, burning and pillaging and stemming the flow of Earth traditions, with little feeling or respect for those involved. Why do people wish to take ownership for something they do not own? Why do they wish to stamp their name on it and ignore indigenous traditions and Earth keepers who have upheld, worked with and guarded the energies for ages before they got there? These atrocities deeply saddened me, and I feel that in honouring their words and energies in this book we are acknowledging their part in this Earth tending.

Close up detail of Eudialyte.

Eudialyte Exercise

Eudialyte strongly links the heart and root together, bridging the gap of what must be done and what your heart wishes to do. This is a simple exercise with the energies of this stone to help you connect your heart and root, and ground yourself in love.

★ Gaze at the Eudialyte photograph at the beginning of this Eudialyte section. Begin to visualize that the golden light codes begin to glow and spin on the page, as they feed energy into the crystals, which begin to glow in all its colours.

★ Breathe in its colours, in and out through your nose and mouth, into your heart and lungs.

★ Allow the colours to move with each inhale into your heart to seat itself there, pooling in light.

★ There it forms a tube of light that arches out through your heart and moves down toward your root.

★ Your red root chakra begins to glow as we bring awareness to it, and welcomes this tube of light in.

★ This connection heart to root is formed and you witness your heart's energies travel down into your root in a whoosh of energy, to support your foundations, your plans, hopes and dreams with love.

★ Finally, imagine a piece of Eudialyte take form in your heart and root at the same time, glowing, spinning and seated happily within you. We thank the medicine of the stones and Sámi elders. Breathe in, magnetizing down more loving energy. Breathe out, grounding yourself in love.

"I am a way-shower stone, helping you discover your purpose. I encourage you to flow with the energies of change. Start something new, embody a new way of being or go on an adventure.

I will lead you through the unknown with grace. When you feel stuck I light a fire within and move you forward; we keep moving together."

Eudialyte

These Herkimers travel across the world with me as a staple in my grids and healing work. They were gifted to me by very dear souls: Caitlin and Gabriella. Thank you for these light beings.

Herkimer Diamond

One of my favourite crystals is the Herkimer Diamond. It holds and embodies such a high percentage of pure, illuminating source light; it is an elevation stone of the highest order.

The way Herkimer Diamonds form is a big reflection of its message: 500 million years ago in pockets of dolostone, Herkimer Diamonds grew unattached to a matrix. Quartz forms surrounded by rock or stone, and Herkimer Diamonds form in pockets free from surrounding matrix stone and so grow points on both ends. These double-terminated points are able to transmit and receive energy through both points, to teach us of balance and the need to both give and take, and are used to facilitate deep meditation states and to expand conscious awareness. Its underlying message is to detach from the 3D false matrices and rise above, illuminating all parts of you.

Herkimer Diamonds are found in Herkimer County in upstate New York, and although they were named after the land, which was in turn named after the war general Nicholas Herkimer, the ancestors and protectors of this stone are the Mohawk Native Americans, known as the "People of the Crystals".

Herkimer Diamonds hold a very high and pure frequency for us and the Earth, and love to charge in the sun.

Herkimer Diamond will show you your inner light, because at times we need reminding how bright we are. Situations can wear us down and we can doubt and question ourselves. It amplifies your heart's fire and reflects such vast light on you that it is hard to ignore. And why should you? Your light is glorious, vibrant and pure, and Herkimer Diamond helps you see your essence and reminds you of the bliss within you. This brings harmony to your space and heart. Herkimer Diamond is a master at this, holding space within and around you for realizations.

This desire to amplify energy does not end with you. Its mission is to help you grow and deepen in your healing practice. Restructuring is a feeling that communicates strongly, wishing to help realign and restructure pathways of light through your third eye and higher chakras, particularly bringing awareness to your soma chakra. The soma chakra is a minor chakra above the third eye, and it is concerned with your connection to the angelic planes for guidance, and when it is imbalanced it directly impacts the ability to co-create your reality. Herkimer Diamond wishes you to look closer at the reality you have created for yourself, or indeed the reality you present to please others. Yes, this is deep work, but Herkimer Diamonds initiations of light come to bring deep shifts of connection to your angels and team of guides, and a connection to the divine healer within. It is important to work with its energy at your third eye or soma chakra and welcome her light streams as they move up through you to your higher chakras, as they call to the angelic kingdoms.

Herkimer Activation

For this activation you will need to connect with the energies of Herkimer Diamond through this crystal grid, or if you have a Herkimer Diamond, place it close to your third eye.

★ Begin by centring and ground yourself with three deep breaths into your heart.
★ Connect with the Herkimer Diamond by gazing at this grid and asking its energy to flow into your third eye. Hold the intent in your heart to work with you to open and expand your higher chakras and all higher channels.
★ Imagine a Herkimer Diamond jumping off the page and into your third eye, where it lights up like a torch, a beacon of light, glowing. It focuses a pure white brilliant ray of diamond light into and through your third eye. Give yourself over to breathing in all of that beam of light into your third eye. Continue to breathe this light into your third eye, welcoming it in, until your third eye is full.
★ Observe as this light flows from your third eye as you guide it upward to your soma chakra, which is located just above the third eye. Connect its diamond light up from your third eye to loop around this energy centre with an infinite loop.
★ Once it is connected in this infinite loop with your third eye, take another strand of diamond light from your third eye and loop it in toward your pineal gland at the base of your brain.
★ Your pineal gland appears like a blue lotus flower, closed. You open each of the petals of this flower with the light of the Herkimer, and the diamond ray enables it to bloom.

This Herkimer Diamond activation moves
to the crown and up, to elevate and expand
the higher and galactic chakras.

★ Once the blue lotus flower is open and glowing, take this stream of pure diamond white light up in an infinite loop of light up to your crown chakra, breathing it into this pure white chakra.

★ You breathe into your crown and feel the swell of diamond light in your crown chakra, growing and glowing and expanding.

★ When your crown feels full of diamond light, let it radiate in its own beam up and out of your crown and into your higher chakra column. Feel the flow of light from the Herkimer Diamond all the way through from the third eye, into your soma, pineal gland and up to your crown, an ever-constant stream of brilliant light that is unifying and expanding all of you.

★ Hold this visual and intention to open all pathways through your higher gateways, in love.

★ You are held in your wholeness in this moment as your breathe it all in.

★ Breathe awareness into your body and heart and we come back to our breath. Ask: what do I wish to reflect to the world? How do I wish to show up?

★ Bask in this diamond glow, breathing it in for as long as you need to recharge and rejuvenate. Then thank Herkimer Diamond for its grace.

"What do you wish to reflect to the world? How do you wish to show up? Bring awareness to patterns replaying so that you can serve yourself and heart in a more efficient way. The energy you give out reflects you and what you stand for, your beliefs and ideas. Perhaps some of those are outdated and on a loop, just playing out through patterns that do not serve you anymore, and all you need to do is bring light and attention to these to start to help them release. It takes courage to commit to growth. What can you surrender to the Earth to be able to move forward now? Hold my energy in your heart, allow my light to shine bright through you, as we work as one to let go, to step up and to release. In that commitment I amplify the intent and we will begin a beautiful journey of connection, to you, to your guides, to the Earth. If you can commit your days and meditations to you, I commit myself to you."

Herkimer Diamond

Grounding crystals grid with polychrome jasper from Madagascar, Red Rock from Kachina Woman, Sedona, haematite quartz from Brazil, Moqui Marbles from Sedona, aragonite copper from the USA and clear quartz and citrine from Brazil.

Sedona Red Rock

The vortexes of red rock in Sedona, Arizona will forever have my heart. Their raw power and majesty stirs something so potent in the heart and waters of the womb. I have the most incredible realization and healing every time I visit. It is a very galactic place and somewhere that sparks so much inspiration, change and healing within. It is, at times, challenging but I have always found the red earth there very supportive.

Three days in Sedona is like months' worth of healing, as the electricity in the land brings forward everything in such an accelerated way. Most recently I visited the Red Rock of Kachina Woman, a sacred place to the Hopi Nation. I saw offerings of flowers strewn around her base and I wondered what I could give back. To which she said:

"You are the offering
Your love is enough
Sing me a song."

Kachina Woman, Boynton
Canyon, Sedona, Arizona.

It reminded me of the words of Apache Tears' guardians: you are the gift, your presence is enough. For what felt like a long while I sang to her, and ancient memories surfaced through my bones of the times we have sung to the stones to attune to their energy fields. And it felt so good to lean into her and be held. Because this is what we used to do in Lemuria: sing to the stones, mountains, rivers and streams. It felt good to open my throat, which in turn opened my creation portal (the womb). Kachina Woman lets me sink deeper into her like a mother would cradle her child, her energy warm and familiar, gentle and tender, holding all parts of me. She referred to herself as a birthing stone, and said to me, "You are pregnant with the universe." Her red rocks speak of enhancing the feminine qualities, inspiration, creativity, flow, inner beauty and how to ground that ancient Earth wisdom through the sacral and root with red flames of fire.

The Kachina Woman embodies the Great Mother energy, one of the stars and Earth, all knowing, a peacekeeper watching over the land here at Boynton Canyon. This canyon is a unified portal of masculine and feminine energy swirls. There is something greater buried beneath her: hidden secrets, Lemurian crystals to connect with, cosmic womb portals and passageways. She holds the great mysteries of this planet. They're all around her in her song. She just asks us to sit still with her to listen and she takes us down into the belly of the mother.

On the way down from her I felt my stomach swell, such strange sensations. It felt as if I was birthing or getting ready to push something out. My womb contracted and out of me came a diamond crystal . . . yes really, there's never a dull moment in my worlds! This was marking the passage of a Lemurian diamond frequency I was carrying to be planted into the Earth, I followed its stream of light down into the Earth grids. This has happened at various points on different sacred lands so it was not a surprise; it is something that is happening more and more as I guide people to the Lemurian energy spots of the Earth to become conscious conductors and transmitters of this Diamond frequency of clarity and pure love.

It always blows me away to get a glimpse of some of the things we are doing. It's like the diagram of the iceberg: only the tip is showing at the surface and so much is unseen under the waters. You have no idea how much work your soul is doing to the support the grids of the Earth, holding balance and harmonizing unseen currents.

Giving offerings at Kachina Woman.

Sedona Red Rock Vision

The Hopi ancestors of this stone appeared in a circle as I sat with the red rock. They seemed lost in prayers, bowing down to the Earth on their knees. The smell of tobacco was thick in the air around them as they communicated with the nature spirits and gave thanks. I didn't think they were aware of my presence, and I was not sure if I was observing a past memory or an imprint on the land, but they seemed to respond to my thoughts because when I asked them if they wished to speak to me, they bowed, head down to the rock and replied that I will get everything I need from the stone. For them to impart the wisdom they get from the stone would be second-hand: why not go directly to her?

They were deep in ceremony and could not speak to me again, and neither did I want to break their focus. So I observed them from a distance and felt the presence of an animal stalk up behind me: a coyote. He silently stopped by my side. "There's nothing wrong," he said, "do not be hurt by their disregard. They are in communion with the great spirit, as are you, and I. We just have our different ways, none of them are wrong. There is so much around us that speaks to us. The Earth talks, we listen." Coyote medicine shows us that when we feel things are backward or going wrong, and when we are hurting, it's actually a healing lesson.

I respected their need for space and prayer time and spoke to the stone herself. She said:

"Celebrate your beauty,
Your inner fire
Your inner caverns and depth
Do not get hung up on the beauty
you have on the outside,
It pales in comparison to the beauty
you have on the inside.
Within you there are caverns of light,
Crystalline streams of love
Fires so golden they set everything aglow
You have this golden fire,
And crystalline river
Let them flow into the Earth.
Nature's beauty resides within you."

I recently led a group to Kachina Woman to give prayers, song and waters to her. Her energy holds and supports life, and her heartbeat is felt so strongly through the red earth, like the beat of a drum. As we sat against her edges she invited us to sink back into her to feel held. The Earth feels quieter here, more peaceful, it's somewhere to go to "run off" the energies the vortex has stirred up within you.

She spoke of the rich tapestry of life, and our place in the weaving of it, being significant in the time we have but also so insignificant in many ways. It's the lessons we learn and pass to our youth that matter.

The Red Rock Birthing Cave, Sedona, Arizona.

Crafting a Talking Stick

Kachina Woman's feminine energies and talk of weaving and creating inspired me to craft a talking stick, which has become an important part of my circles, retreats and gatherings. I have always loved the concept of the talking stick, which is used by many indigenous communities. It is an ancient communication tool, used when gathered in ceremony, council circles, for cultural events or storytelling circles. The person holding the stick has the right to speak, while all others listen respectfully.

I wanted to create a talking stick that could also become a symbol of courage and bravery. I came up with the idea of having each person in the circle who shared a story, and their truth and vulnerability, to tie a thread around the talking stick so that it is a reminder to those who hold it, including myself, that it's OK to be vulnerable. Every time I look at my talking stick and the colourful threads tied around it, I am reminded of the strong women who share their deepest feelings and it makes me smile. It's also become a symbol of togetherness, support and community. When someone new holds the stick it is my wish that they feel the support of their sisters, brothers and ancestors through it and it gives them the strength they need.

My talking stick is made of some old oak root I found on a walk through the woods. I'd held the intention to find something special from nature to use for this purpose when I'd gone out. This stick is now adorned with found feathers and bells, shells and oak moss. I chose two crystals for it: an amethyst point and a piece of blue kyanite, because blue kyanite resonates with the throat chakra and helps open the voice up.

My talking stick travels with me. The threads on it have been tied on by the women who have been vulnerable and shared their stories.

You will need

* A stick to decorate
* A stain of your choice (optional)
* Glue or thin wire to secure the stones
* Crystals you might like to decorate it with
* Thread in different colours if you wish to wrap the stick
* Coloured acrylic paint
* Paintbrush
* Faux leather or suede string (optional)
* Other ideas for adornments: Feathers, seed pods, shells, beads and bells

* Take some time to find the right stick for your project. If you put it out to the universe the right one will find you. The type of wood you find will be symbolic. For example, mine is oak, which symbolizes strength and courage.
* When you have found it, you can prepare it by sawing off any unwanted branches and peeling off any bark, and finally, sanding it down. This is your opportunity to connect with the energies of the natural world, the trees and ask them for support and connection. At this point you can stain it if you wish, but I chose to keep it untreated and natural.
* Once you have taken time preparing the stick comes the fun part: the collecting and decorating. It can be as simple or elaborate as you wish. I glued and tied the crystals onto mine, and wrapped threads around them to secure them. Then I painted on symbols meaningful to me. You can do the same.

"Your life is a tapestry,

Beauty woven into every thread

The tapestry is woven across
lives and dimensional planes

Your legacy is love

Each thread of love is woven into the ether."

Sedona Red Rock

The limestones Temple of Muyil, Mexico.

Limestone

Many of the sacred sites of the world are built using Limestone: the pyramids of Egypt, the step pyramid of Chichén Itzá, the Acropolis in Athens and the Colosseum in Rome are just some of them, and all of these structures have survived thousands of years, standing the test of time.

Limestone is a strong and beautiful building material that we use in current buildings today. It is made of ancient animal shells and corals, calcium, aragonite, magnesium, clay and sand, and is a sedimentary rock that forms in shallow, calm and warm waters. I have found myself being called to the Yucatan many times in the past couple of years, and even to specific Limestones sites within the Yucatan to create crystal grids there and anchor love frequencies. A site that intrigued me and brought on so many visions was the Well of Magicians at Chichén Itzá, Mexico. This was a sacred oracle site and a big open cenote they called a well where they would communicate with the underworld.

I sat at its walls, and my son dropped to the ground instantly as if in a trance, silently connecting, and I heard the Limestone chanting, the voices of the Mayan shamans still reverberating off the stones. It was so strong it felt like I was there in a ceremony with them. It made me think about how the stones hold prayers, sounds and voices all as imprints and for those sensitive enough to hear them. Often people are taught to "program" or "clear" crystals of energies before they work with them, and I thought of this concept, "These Limestones did not need to be 'wiped' or cleared of energies." They took care of themselves. They hold the imprints and voices because it is important to, because they are record keepers. Formed over thousands of years, they record the progress of the Earth and humanity. Limestone is a very porous stone that absorbs water, and it is this property in the physical, which is reflected in the spiritual. It absorbs, records and also transmutes and cleanses energies. I have always known the stone harness and hold so much for us, as well as graciously offering their healing energies to us, because they are our teachers.

A Limestone Guardian who stands watch in the Oracle's Cave in Delphi, Greece confirmed this feeling to me. This old mossy stone has seen many things. It is in the cave halfway up Mount Parnassus, and the Limestone cave itself is ancient and full of mystery, a home of the "Melissae", the bee priestess and oracles, and more recently Pan is remembered here. The cave is vast, but it was this guardian stone standing close to the centre point that drew me in. It had many faery portals and gnomes around it, holding space. I could feel it was once part of the cave structure as a giant stalagmite. It hummed so loudly, vibrating around the space, a masculine energy, and when I touched it many elemental beings poked their heads around to look at me, half trying to hide, but intrigue getting the better of them. They all told me that they are the keepers of this space, that over time people had come and created them into form and shape. They spoke of the alchemy that was performed in this space, and the creation energy that is strong in here, as the priestess and divine birth vessels anchored creation codes through their wombs. An elderly male being took the lead to speak to me. He was tall and lean, with spindly limbs like spider's and a large, long nose. He came out from behind the rock, a spokesperson.

"We come through the rock, and it acts as a portal through to inner Earth where many of us reside. There are many entry points on the grid, at points of high energy like this where we can step through. The rocks and rock guardians pin down large energies that become powerful swirls of energy that we can bounce through."

He heard my thought before I had a chance to finish it:

"Yes, the mountains hold and amplify a lot of energies, and yes they become inter-dimensional portals for larger beings. What can we help you with?"

I said, "I am just observing the energies of this space and wanting to connect deeper to the Limestone." He found this curious, and scratched his head, looking slightly confused.

"But you are part of the Limestone, so to connect with the Limestone is to connect deeper with yourself. You are creation energy, you hold creation energies in you.

"I have watched souls come here and create magic. The stones have watched. These energies of creation

impregnate the space. The stones here absorb them and hold them and they are waiting for you to tap into them.

"The stones are here to help you open to the creative energies you hold within you, and to realize your true potential as a creator being. This stretches to the reality you live in. If you are having a hard time, create a new reality, paint it into existence in the Limestone caves. Where better to create than the belly of the Earth?"

Stone guardian at the cave of the oracles in Greece.

I have had many expansive and magical stories of the Limestone I wish to share with you, and talking about them is where I come alive, so I hope you can be there and feel this through my words and photographs. The most important was the experience I had at the Maya temple space called "Muyil" in Tulum. This Limestone complex sprawls through the jungle and is a deeply feminine vibration. I was walking through the site, listening to the stones that wanted me to touch them, taking my large Lemurian Quartz amplifier and placing it in sequence on certain rocks, and tapping on them. I came upon a step pyramid structure, and as I connected with it, angelic language poured from my lips, as it often does when I'm in a flow state, and the whole complex started to glow a beautiful rosy pink, its rays shining out in all directions. This prompted me to excitedly call to my friend, "It's pink, it's all pink."

The stones and guardians instructed me to walk around the pyramid clockwise, tapping on certain spots with my Quartz, and as I did the whole thing came apart from the top to the base in my mind's eye. From the centre point a radiant pink light beam and two beings rose from it. They had elongated heads, crystalline in structure, which glowed with pure diamond light. The main thing I noticed was that they were wearing flowing watery robes and a beautiful headdress of incredible coloured feathers that fell from behind their ears all the way down their back. In the centre of the pink ray I saw was a giant Rose Quartz crystal skull. Within a moment there was a whoosh of light and the beings disappeared.

I had just watched a changing of the guards. The beings were protectors of the site that were removing their energy. This is something I have witnessed over and over at many sacred sites: a change of guardians where the energy or timeline reaches a certain point. I continued to move around the temple building and stood in front of it. Here, I felt all my timelines at once and looked down at my feet and they were mine but also someone else's. I was an elder Mayan woman at this site in the past, praying to the heavens and Earth in union. I felt this was the most sacred place in the whole of the site. I knew nothing of this place, only what I felt and saw. A serendipitous moment was when I came across a small plaque talking about the site, calling it "The Pink Temple", which was the main religious site of the complex, and was used for the shamans to heal and give ceremonies. This made me smile and affirmed what I saw. The pink ray of divine love was anchored deeply at this spot.

The Mayan guardians communicated with me that I must bring people back to this site to grid crystal skulls. So a few months later I had organized a retreat and was back with twelve women sitting in a circle each with a large pink crystal skull I had requested they bring. We gridded these and dropped into our hearts to hold space for energies to move through us. The next time I went there fell on a solar eclipse without my consciously planning it, and I took another group of twelve women there. It was more angelic this time, and we gridded rose quartz, opalite and lemurian quartz with the same intent to tune in to the pink ray and swap frequency coding from our heart with the Earth. I returned a final and third time six months later, which fell on another solar eclipse. Again, this was not planned.

The last important story of the magic of Limestone lies in a pilgrimage I did to the south of France to be in the divine feminine energies of the Saint Baume, and the Limestone caves where Mary Magdalene spent the final 30 years of her life. This story will resonate with those who connect deeply to the Goddess Isis, Artemis and those of the Magdalene lineage.

I had heard whispers of a cave of eggs that was partway down the mountain: a fertility site of the goddess, and very different from her grotto at the top of the mountain where you can sit in on religious ceremonies. I didn't hold expectations to find it, because I heard that it did not show itself to everyone, but I put it

Rose quartz crystal skull connection at Muyil,
Mexico, anchoring the ray of divine love
and activating the wisdom of the crystals
skulls through their Maya protectors.

out there to the goddess that I would love to connect with their
energies and stones there. I was so excited to see what flowers
grew there, to meet them and to speak to the stones.

The first day we climbed the mountain and felt the feminine
flow and her whispers in every rock, tree and flower. The
energy of the land and forest there felt high-vibrational and
joyous, and when you tuned in it took you to your higher
heart and upland out of the crown chakra. It had a feel of
acceleration and soul growth.

I reached the grotto and sat in the energies of the larger cave
where I touched and pressed my head against the Limestone.
It showed me the crystalline grid of that space and how they

Solar eclipse 2024 gathering at Muyil's "Pink Temple", anchoring and embodying the pink ray of divine love with rose quartz, lemurian quartz and selenite.

held the energy there. I could see and feel the ways the Magdalene priestess had co-created this high-vibrational template with the rocks and mountain. It appeared like a web of light mapped out through the space. I could see the points of connection glow and things shifted and moved, breathing. There was an understanding of the way the mountain's energy shifts and changes to accommodate the movement and flow of energies, of people, in and out. The co-creation between person and nature was felt so strongly it reminded me of the Limestone message in the caves of Delphi.

We went on a mission to find the Cave of Eggs. There were so many white butterflies flying in my path. I just followed them and it led us to the top of the mountain. I picked some mountain lavender on the way up and spent some peaceful moments at the top. Then I was instructed by my guides to hold my Quartz. There was a reason I had to find the top: it was to anchor completely through the whole, from the top, down through the caves and into the Earth. On the way down the sun started to set, and we came so close to the Cave of Eggs I could feel it, but it got too dark to continue. So we went home happy, and the next day we had to fly home. It happened to be Mary Magdalene's feast day. I just didn't feel it was time to go; this cave wanted us to find it, so we extended our stay and that day we went back to the mountain to climb it. This time it flowed and we met some glorious ladies who helped us find the way, and like a magical fairy tale a trail of rose petals appeared that helped us.

When we found the cave it was incredible. The Limestone in it felt holy, with an aura of the sacred. There was a man and his son outside the entrance and he looked at me: I must have looked fairly normal as I smiled at him. He said, "There is lots of chanting and smoke going on down there, just so you know." I caught the meaning: he was warning me. I'd heard a whisper from the priests of the church in the grotto above that they did not like this space and said it was where witchcraft was done, and by that they meant the ceremony this man was describing. Little did he know. I smiled and thanked him, before I stood in front of the entrance and sang to the stones, imagining his face at that moment of realization that I was there to sit with the goddess too.

It was cold and damp and a really slippery climb down to the small inner chamber. There were people who cleared out

Connecting with the energies of
Sainte-Baume, the south of France.

and made room for us, and I found myself with three others, one we had met on the hike and a Danish woman who was in silent prayer. We gave offerings, sang and held hands, and there was more light language coming from me and visions flowed in of the priestess here before, who had shapeshifted and created from the womb in this space. The cave, I learnt, was a sacred space for fertility rites even before the Magdalene, and I imagine it was visited by the priestess of Artemis and many others. The Limestone did not speak to me, it just listened to us, offering connections to the past through every breath in its inner chamber.

Limestone enhances and facilitates deep healing, especially the Limestone at sacred sites that hold so many energies of love. They speak of their wish to record Earth's

We found the Cave of Eggs, an ancient site of worship to the goddess. Before the Magdalene connection it was a place of pilgrimage of the cult of Artemis, for fertility and for many others before them.

imprints, cycles and history. They capture the voices of those who have spoken in and around them, and those who have climbed within their caves, sung to them in thanks or climbed their dizzying heights. As the original record keepers of this planet, Limestone is happy to share its recordings, and if you place your hand on them and ask, they have a wealth of healing information locked within waiting to share. It enhances purification and healing with a quiet, steady, grounding energy that finds you now to say:

"You are a crystalline record keeper, and everything is recorded within your cells and crystals of your water. I stand still observing, never able to change or affect anything that passes. But small moments create big ripples. I ask that you take the role of observer more seriously. Try not to attach too much to thoughts and actions, and just observe them like I do. Try to be less reactive and take pause to witness."

Limestone

Through my interactions at many sites and stone circles I have found that the stones have many guardians: those who have lived and spent time there through the ages who loved and dedicated themselves to the space, and who can still speak through the stone. Other times the crystal has one very strong over-lighting guardian energy that wishes to impart important wisdom, which is very true in the case of eudialyte and labradorite. In essence the stones are transmitters, and all stones are record keepers.

Working with the Limestone in a
circle in the Yucatan, Mexico.

In the belly of the Cave of Eggs offering
love and devotion in the darkness.

The Medicine of Limestone

This connection is simple: the Limestone caverns of the Earth wish to greet you and ask of you and only you: what are you creating, birthing and bringing to life?

You don't need anything for this meditation, just an open mind and heart. To connect with the Limestone cave, gaze at the image of the Magdalene Cave of Eggs before you begin.

★ Take some time to breathe three long, grounding breaths into your body as we invoke the energies of the Limestone caverns and their priestess guardians over time.

★ Hold the intention to connect with the creation energy in your heart and womb/ sacral chakra. Place your left hand on your heart, and your right hand on your womb/sacral chakra.

★ Take the time to paint the vision of a beautiful cave shaped like you, perhaps taking yourself to the Cave of Eggs. You stand at the entrance: in front of you is darkness, mystery and promise. You feel a cool breeze whip through your hair. You place your hand on the side of the Limestone entrance.

★ Feeling the texture of the stone and its rough edges, you send your heart's light through your arms and out of your hands into the stone to connect. It feels your love and warmth.

★ You ask permission to enter and co-create with its energies.

★ You enter the cave, stepping down into the dark space, feeling the damp in the air. Take a breath in. Its energies hum.

★ You continue to walk down deeper into its belly. In the distance you see light and you follow it, climbing down and into an inner chamber.

★ This light is a small fire with offerings to the goddess and roses strewn across the floor.

★ You step lightly across the threshold and sit with your back against the cold Limestone in this small inner chamber.

★ Breathe.

★ The spirit of place makes itself known, with many of the women that have come to this space before you. The rock guardians ask you: "What do you wish to birth into this world and what do you wish to create?"

★ You speak what you wish to create into existence, out loud now, into this space where the stones are listening and the energies are strong to help you manifest and co-create light.

★ You feel your wishes, hopes and dreams dance around this space, in the air, through the fire, and permeating through every stone around you. You smile and your heart smiles with recognition and love.

★ The rock guardians hold your wishes with the prayers of those before you.

★ Here in this sacred space, the belly of the mother, surrounded by Limestone walls, you sing your visions and creations into existence, and they will be made manifest. You lean into the fire and offer something in thanks, some flowers, or perhaps some beech seed pods, feathers or herbs.

★ Once you have impregnated this sacred space with your love, you can get up to leave, thanking the energies. Slowly make your way up out of the inner chamber, following the light until you reach the entrance where the sunlight greets your beautiful face. You breathe in its warm golden glow, and know you are safe, you are held and you are loved dearly.

"You are a crystalline record keeper, and everything is recorded within your cells and crystals of your water. I stand still observing, never able to change or affect anything that passes, but small moments create big ripples. I ask that you take the role of observer more seriously. Try not to attach too much to thoughts and actions, and just observe them like I do. Try to be less reactive and take pause to witness."

Limestone

This is my Sphalerite skull, who unlocks ancient
energy streams within you. Gaze upon her and into
her eyes and be open to what she has to say to you.

Sphalerite

Sphalerites formed with a variety of minerals such as fluorite, pyrite, galena, dolomite, quartz and calcite. And depending on the iron content, they can come in silver, grey, red, black, yellow, brown, green and colourless.

Ernst Friedrich Glocker named them in 1847, and the name comes from the Greek word "Sphaleros", which can mean "treacherous" and or "deceiving", as Sphalerite contains so many minerals that at times it is difficult to identify. Its special grounding properties have something to do with the combination of minerals within it.

A special Sphalerite crystal skull found me when I was writing a book about the divine mother and the priestess of Isis and Magdalene lineages. I sat with it and it brought through a strong stream of divine feminine energy that took the form of a young Magdalene priestess who spoke French to me and called herself "Magdalena of the Mountain". She called me her *soeur de coeur*, which translates as "soul sister" or "sister of the heart". Then came a beautiful journey with this stone spanning years of learning, remembering and writing, which weaves in with my trip to her mountain and limestone's story in the previous chapter.

What I have learnt is that Sphalerite is an opening of ancestral wisdom, to support intense and beautiful spiritual growth and soul evolution. It offers a huge level of detail and information while grounding this down through the heart, which allows us to embody our truth and remember lessons of unified love we have learned in the past. It is a past life connection and a gift enhancer. Sphalerite also is a connection of ancient energy streams, above and below the Earth. She magnetizes to you that which you need in the moment to support your healing journey, and her energy presents as a mystic grandmother energy, grounded in her approach and balanced energy. She is a teacher stone: lean in to her and offer her your worries and she will give you a higher perspective. She is a wonderful stone for guidance when embarking on a spiritual journey. Through Sphalerite, you can connect with the teachers and scribes of your past if you hold it and ask it to show you the ancient streams of consciousness you have worked with. They will present themselves and the re-learning begins as she will re-open those streams to run through you once more.

A stone with very powerful grounding properties, Sphalerite is about Earth anchoring through the lower chakras: the sacral, root and earth star chakra. Working with it will help you re-group your energy, re-grounding and energizing your subtle bodies. The strong earthy energies within it will balance you if you feel overwhelmed, dizzy or lightheaded from any high-vibrational spiritual work. Its flow of energy will also ground the nervous system, helping with over-stimulation, which supports people who are neurodiverse, such as people with ADHD, holding you through feelings of exhaustion, building you up so

My Sphalerite skull sat on top of Sainte-Baume mountains in the south of France.

you can feel strong and become more resilient. The full-bodied grounding it will offer you through your chakras will bring empowerment, focus and drive that you never knew you had and it taps into the inner reserves of strength, and courage to believe in yourself.

Sphalerite speaks on her earthly missions during this ascension cycle:

"My energy has the ability to weave high streams of information, vibration, sound and light into the body, where they will then be woven in with the very deepest parts of your being to your core, to bring feeling and light to the dark spaces.

"See my energy form as a grounding web of light that surrounds you from above, like a net that will gather up all scattered energy and merge them back into your body, mind and soul.

"There is nothing more grounding than love, as we connect in with the love Mother Earth has to offer together. All of your elemental fragments, eleven light codes and faery light will be magnetized back to you in an elemental reclaiming.

"Hold me in your hands and in your heart, as I activate in connection with your heart's intent and call back energy like a magnet."

Meditation to Connect With Sphalerite

Sphalerite generally has a strong current of action that will connect and move within all of the chakras under the heart. Place it at your root to anchor and ground all cosmic and Earth uploads/downloads. It wishes to be held and worked with to support activation of the hands and palm chakras. Work with it on your womb to support a grounding of sovereignty, queen codes and empowerment.

You will need a piece of Sphalerite if you have one – if not you can connect through the crystal skull photograph.

* Take some time to gaze at the photograph of the Sphalerite crystal skull. Notice its colours, its caves, its textures, imagining what it feels like in your hands, as you connect fully with it through its eyes.
* Welcome its energy in as it glows and moves into your body.
* Ask it to open ancient wisdom within and through you, and ask it to connect you to elemental aspects of yourself and to re-open dormant ancient energy streams.
* Receive its energy as it wakes up to you and lights up in your mind's eye. You may hear it, feel it vibrate in your hands or see its colours lighting up in your third eye.
* As you open your heart and send your heart's light around and into this stone, it hears you and absorbs it on connection.
* You allow its aura to fill with its colours, and you breathe them now into your body, into your hands, into your heart, into your lungs. You allow its energy to stream into your body where it wishes to go, as this red, brown and black light runs through

you, observing where it goes. It is not attaching, so let go of any limiting beliefs.

★ You ask it: "What is your medicine for me?"

★ Pieces of you come home now, magnetizing back to you as if they were pieces of armour, parts of your lightbody, your shield.

★ Sphalerite's protective light fills your aura and radiates around you, inside and out. Taking back all body parts, all soul fragments as they emerge in light back through your energy field. Sphalerite's energy is like a teacher, there to support this piecing back of light.

★ You observe yourself, your expanded being, rebuilding and strengthening.

★ Pieces clicking back together like a jigsaw as Sphalerite's energy fills in the gaps, from the top of your lightbody to bottom, filling and holding.

★ We are the ancient ones, rising as one.

★ And so we bring awareness back into our body and heart as we thank Sphalerite for its medicine and healing balm.

★ We breathe into our lightbody deeply, feel its expansion and flex our light, knowing we are re-claiming so much not just for us but for our soul group, monadic group and ancestors.

★ Take some time to breathe and re-ground in all the ways that feel good to you.

"You can't run before you can walk …

The honouring of energy is important.
Do not rush on – stop, hold and honour
the wisdom you are receiving."

Sphalerite

A large Fulgurite formed in the Sahara desert.

Fulgurite

I have always been intrigued by Fulgurite, and how it is formed when lightning hits the Earth at great speed and a temperature beyond 1,800°C/3,270°F. The sand or soil it strikes makes silica (quartz) sand or rock fuse to make a tube structure holding the raw elemental energy of lightning.

The Latin word *fulgur* means "lightning", and these Fulgurite tubes are the most incredibly "electric" energy I have ever worked with. They are incredible for helping you manifest and shake up your energy field to clear and expand you. My ancestors told me that Fulgurite is a gift from the thunder gods.

When I found my piece of Fulgurite, I instinctively moved it to my lips to blow through it, and it made my lips tingle on contact. For a stone to have such an instant effect you get a glimpse of its power. The ancestors say it is a gift from the thunder gods to the Earth, as a tool of power and connection to the Earth and sky. It holds and channels a strong, charged electrical current, which will shake you up from the inside, bringing cellular rejuvenation. I always look for Fulgurite that has an open tube as personally I find that movement of energy through it most powerful.

A Fulgurite crystals grid around a lava stone skull, with moldavite, golden lydian tektite and garnets from Mali. Created with the intent to provide clearing and elevation. My Lemurian crystal skull is breathing life into it.

A Fulgurite Vision

I sat with my Fulgurite and called forward the ancestral energy that protected and worked with it, and an elderly man appeared. He sat cross-legged with a piece of Fulgurite to his lips. It was black and rough, made of crystallized soil, and it looked like he was playing it like an instrument, like a snake charmer, calling something up and out of the Earth. I knew he was journeying because his eyes were closed, and I could feel his energy wandering through the etheric. I got closer to him and heard the prayers he was whispering silently to the wind. At his side on the ground was a small pouch with more Fulgurites in it.

He opened his eyes and looked at me as he felt my energy shift closer to him, and he followed my gaze down to the bag of Fulgurite. He told me that he collects them, and that they are powerful tools to call energies through the Earth. These energies can be worked with to bring people what they need. They create abundance currents and harness electro-magnetic energies to harness and conduct prayers. He led me to a clearing on the Earth, where the floor was bare and well worn, just soil. Here he took the Fulgurite out of his pouch and moved around the soil in a circle, placing a Fulgurite upright in the soil like an antenna. I watched him go about his work, and it seemed methodical in a way. He knew where they needed to go and they ended up making a circle. He then blew into each one to connect them to the Earth and wake up the energies.

I asked him, "What do we do next?"

He said, "Now we wait."

So we sat and watched them as they called up streams of energies through the Earth and moved electricity through the ground until it became one big glowing channel of light. And as the light connected in a web of light, my guide started to sing and chant to welcome in the new.

This was a beautiful masterpiece of energy playing out in front of my eyes and perfectly highlighted the ways we can work with these stones to connect to the Earth. They can clear dense energy from the Earth grids and charge them with bolts of energy to reawaken old dormant energy streams, enhancing your connection to the Earth. The ancestors worked with the energies of Fulgurite to predict the future and enhance the abilities of divining rod.

How to Work With the Medicine of Fulgurite

★ If you have a piece of Fulgurite, activate it by placing your lips to the end of it and blow into it. This is to stir up its electric energies.

★ Fulgurite spirals energy in and out, so connect with the spiral and move it through your chakras, front to back, and up and down the spine.

★ Go inside it, hold yourself in a tube of Fulgurite in your third eye and paint it into existence. This chamber of charged energy with support for awakening of your systems and consciousness.

Me and Mazebah, the owner of the store Crystal Matrix in Mount Shasta. He is a guardian and his store is a gateway to many crystalline dimensions. We had the most joyful conversations about orks and elves in star languages.

Holding the largest Fulgurite I have ever seen.

Ritual to Manifest With Fulgurite

You will need a piece of Fulgurite, making sure the tube is open and intact.

* Before we begin, I wish for you to take a moment to write down what you are calling in now at this time. What do you wish for? It could be something for you, or something for the collective.
* Get comfortable and start to ground all your energy and thoughts into your body with your breath. Call all of your energy back to you so you can be fully present in this moment.
* Hold the Fulgurite in your hands and to your heart, and ask it to open all of the channels of abundance and love in your body.
* Then call onto your heart a visual of what you wish to create. Hold it there with love, knowing it is happening, and it has happened. Hold how it makes you feel in your heart, and use all your senses to really feel it in all of your cells.
* Paint the picture fully in your mind's eye, and hold the happiness you feel in your heart, feeling it in every cell.
* Keep the vision clearly in your mind as you meditate, keeping all thoughts positive.
* Feel yourself smiling from within and imagining the Fulgurite glowing golden in your hand as it hears you and activates your breath.
* Hold your Fulgurite in your hand, roll it from one hand to the other, becoming aware of the power that it holds within it as it starts to vibrate in your hand.
* Feel waves of gratitude for what you are about to receive.

★ If you want, speak aloud to the universe, making a statement about what it is that you are asking for.

★ As you place the Fulgurite to your heart, this feeling of gratitude lights up your heart, allowing its spiralling currents to enter there. It merges with your heart's threefold flame, which is blue, magenta and gold, as it amplifies and surges through all of our hearts' chambers. Here, the manifesting is taking place. This energetic power flows through the body and you can feel it as it centres fully in the heart and higher heart chakra.

★ We hold this warm glow in our heart as a seed of light, which begins to grow and bloom. We then take this seed of light, this vision, and held up into our breath.

★ Place your Fulgurite to your lips and blow your vision, hopes and dreams as a seed of light out to the universe. As you exhale your intent through the tube, imagine it takes on the form of a lightning bolt, following its luminous glow as it streaks through the universe connecting with the source of all that is.

★ Follow this stream of light as it moves up through the skies to connect in with the golden unity grid above the planet and merge with it.

★ We thank all of the air sylphs for supporting us in our prayers and intentions. We thank the Mother Earth, the plants, minerals and the shamanic energies of Fulgurite.

★ Next, take the Fulgurite down to the ground and blow down to the Earth, touching the Fulgurite down to the Earth to impregnate it within the heaven and Earth, for all to hear. Feel, see and be with your wishes and prayers for the future. Travel down deep into the Earth to anchor: as above and so below.

"I will help you process rapid change through your body into the higher realms and fields. My gift is to speed up the process of release at the optimum rate for you, while keeping a harmonious balance within you, so you can evolve and grow spiritually.

To achieve your optimum potential in the fastest space of time for you, I speed up the particles, atoms and spaces between atoms. I wake up dormant cells and infrastructures of the lightbody that have been there since the dawn of your time on Earth, those systems that you stopped working with as specific programming to the mental field came in during Atlantis.

I am filled with divine light.
I radiate and enhance it, anchoring it into your lightbody fully."

Fulgurite

Crystals grid from Stromatolite central stone with jasper crystal skull, pietersite and Stromatolite tumble stones and pyrite. This grid supports connection with the ancestors and grounding ancestral wisdom.

Stromatolite

Stromatolite has ancient origins. It is one of the first living organisms on Earth, formed over 3.7 billion years ago. Made of layers of cyanobacteria (algae) with ancient sedimentary rock, it is formed of single-celled photosynthesizing microbe, which were the first cells to photosynthesis and produce oxygen.

From the very first moment I engaged with Stromatolite, it took me back to the Triassic era and showed me lush green fern-like plants thriving all over the Earth. Its energy is slow and steady, and comes in layers, each as unique as the next. Some are fast in pace and some are slower and denser, and that is a nod to the way it has formed, encased and fossilized. At times its energy feels trapped through layers that you may have to work to get at, but it's waiting, eager to work with you. It's a stone of patience, and works in an organic way through layers of you. It's happy to sit back and help you be calm and relaxed, but if you wish to push forward it will listen, as it is very adaptable. It will help you to simplify problems and worries, stripping it all back to the bones: the trauma, fear and pain through the emotional and mental layers, to the simple facts and basics of life.

As you work with it, it opens deeper. Nothing can be hidden from it, and it exposes and breaks imposed structures that do not serve your highest good, and at the same time gently holds you. It's such a strong, grounding Earth stone. It holds the eternal wisdom of Mother Nature that emanated billions of years ago. It takes you back to the beginning of life, connecting you to the primordial state of Earth, when the energy was more pure, in an innocent infantile state. It's in this state of purity that it can reconnect us with the wisdom of the ancients, and by activating our cellular memory, Stromatolite brings its energy into the cells to activate these dormant memories. I was lucky to connect with some ancient living Stromatolites in a Mayan reserve in Tulum, and it was lovely to feel its pure life-force energy first hand.

How to Work With Stromatolite's Energy

Placed at the root, Stromatolite's energy will harmonize and activate higher frequencies to move through you and into the Earth. It works to fill your cells with its light to be able to ground higher vibrations.

Place Stromatolite on your third eye to bring calm to a racing mind. It works to bring grounding and cooling energy to all parts of your body and it will slow and ground your thoughts so you can rest and be still.

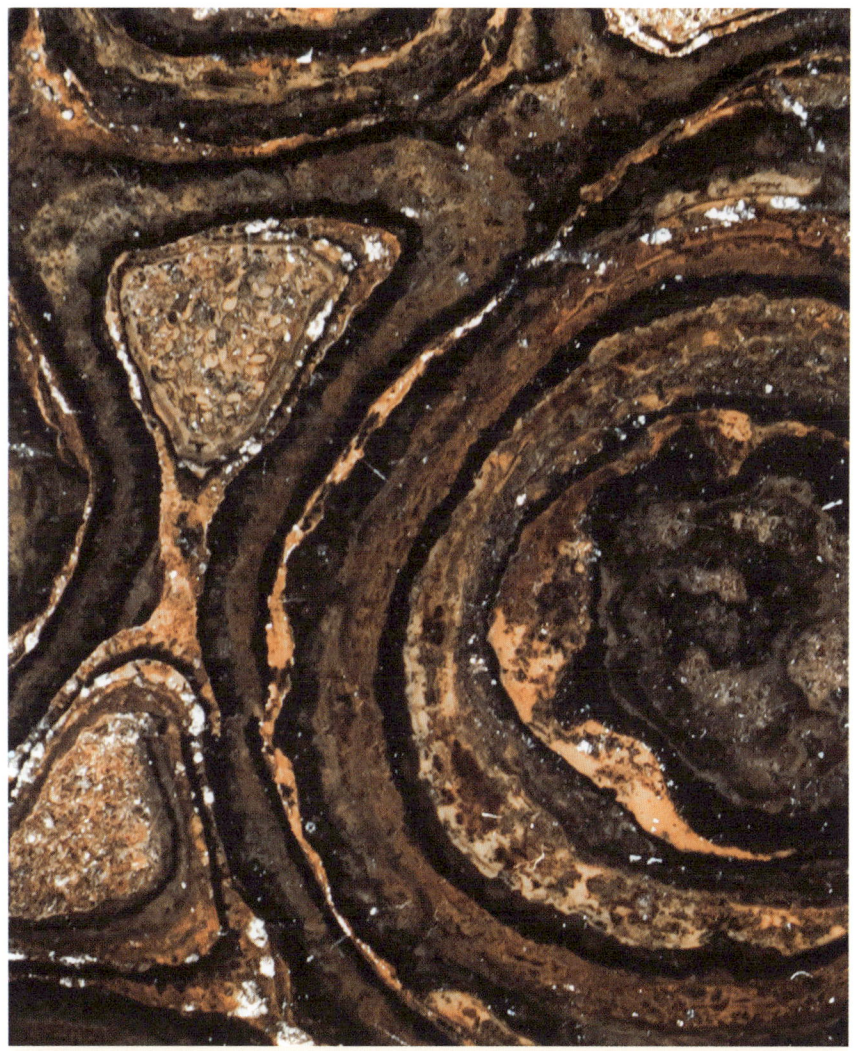

A close-up of Stromatolite.

Ritual to Slow Down With Stromatolite

Take some time to gaze at Stromatolite's brown layers through my photographs to form a connection with the stone.

You will need some music and scented candles or incense.

* Find a calm moment in the day where you can dedicate 15 minutes to yourself and to surrendering and stillness. Lay down or sit comfortably in a peaceful space where you will not be disturbed, and play some music or light some relaxing scented candles or incense in the room.
* Breathe three rounds of breath in a slow and comfortable way.
* Call Stromatolite to your mind. Imagine it floating in your space, connecting with your lightbody; notice its brown layers and how its energy feels to you.
* Begin to breathe in its deep brown glow, letting its energy enter your body in waves.
* As you continue to breathe it down into the depths of you and each of your lower chakras, you notice your heartbeat on the inbreath.
* With the next deep breath in, Stromatolite's energy will attune you to the heartbeat of the Earth. You will hear the Earth's low, deep thuds.
* Consciously slow down your heartbeat. Slow down your energy centres, feeling all of your muscles release and let go a little more as you sink into the Earth.
* Focus on this connection with the Earth's heartbeat for as long as you need to feel calm and present.

Holding a Vision of 5D Earth With Stromatolite

You will need Stromatolite – if not you can connect through the photographs in this book.

* Take a moment to get seated comfortably, and take your time to gaze at Stromatolite and welcome its energy into you, letting it know that you are ready to work with it.
  Ask it to open up and work with you for a deeper connection to the Earth.
* Begin by taking three deep breaths to ground and centre your energy. Close your eyes and bring your awareness to your breath. Feel the breath touching the tips of your nostrils, passing through the nasal passages into the lungs, diaphragm, abdomen and all the way out.
* Begin by calling in your layers of protection.
* Visualize golden infinity loops arching down like a bridge from their source, like a golden sun above your head. They link down through each higher chakra into your crown and through your chakras until it passes out of your base chakra into your earth star chakra and then into the core of the Earth.
* Next we connect it with your tube of light, bringing it up around you, your portal space of light that protects and holds you, as you rise up to connect with your higher self.
* Take a few moments to breathe into your heart, visualizing your threefold flame, the magenta pink, royal blue and gold spiralling together inside your heart as you find yourself standing within it and breathing it in. Do this for as long as

you need to, and bring full focus to your heart as this flame expands and open your heart, fully, through all chambers.

★ We bring awareness to the Stromatolite in your hand, as you feel your palm chakras open to receive waves of its thick brown energy, moving in through your hands, up your arms to where in the body they need to go. Be free with this. Do not attach; just allow this current to flow through you to settle into the parts of you and your body you need to assist with grounding.

★ As its brown energy settles in your body, it begins to multiply in waves through every cell, every atom and the space between cells in turn. It brings grounding, slowing your energy field down.

★ We move down to your base chakra: it has opened and expanded so much since the last session with Fulgurite. We now ask Stromatolite's energy to harmonize and ground all vibrations running through you, allowing its energy to gather and sit in your base chakra. It then moves down through you, down through your legs and feet to move out of you and connect in with your earth star chakra, re-opening and strengthening new pathways of light.

★ Now your energy is grounded within your body wholly. You can connect with the heartbeat of the Earth. As you feel the Earth beneath your feet, it beats through your feet and into your body, into each cell as you come into alignment with the Earth's heartbeat, and moves up to your heart. Your heartbeat is beating in unison with the Earth. You become aware of the copper at your feet as you welcome its warm copper glow in through your open feet chakras, to flow into your body and amplify and carry all currents of energy in a more efficient way.

★ The crystal grids of the Earth begin to rise up from the crystal core, iridescent diamond and white light reaching up, moving through the layers of Earth to greet you, to surround and hold you. They draw closer to merge with your light field. As you breathe in the crystalline grid to your lightbody it pulses and connects with all cells, rippling light through you.

★ The golden unity grid of the Earth begins to descend to greet you, moving down from the heavens to swaddle over you like a blanket, coming close and connecting with your lightbody and the crystalline grid around you.

★ We bring our left hand holding the Stromatolite to our heart, connecting with its brown energy once again, welcoming the flow directly into our heart, and holding in our mind's eye and in our heart a vision for the new Earth. We experience the Earth through Stromatolite's frequency. It holds ascension keys and an energetic signature of pure times, where the energies of the land were clear, the water and seas were crystalline, and there was no pollution. Huge green vibrant ferns grow now around you, and crisp clear air surrounds you and fills your lungs. Everything feels luminous and sparkling. The sun above your head beams down warmth and light of a magical property, and you receive it into your body.

★ You begin to feel your heart pulse in gratitude. We are re-lighting the energy of the ancient days, the original pure state of this Earth. It is this vision we hold in our hearts when working with this crystal. We send that love, awe and gratitude to the crystalline grids surrounding our body, pulsing that light out in waves to connect to the Earth. Holding the beauty and love of this new Earth we are co-creating within our hearts. We thank all crystals and crystal guardians of this course and send love and gratitude back to the crystalline grids and unity grid of this planet.

★ Spend as much time as you wish connecting with the love you feel and sending it into the Earth's grids. You may ask the air and Earth dragons to quicken the flow up, asking them to carry and amplify these wishes and energies so more can feel them.

★ Begin to come back to your breath. Connect in with the flowing golden infinite symbols that link through your chakras and down through you into the Earth's core as you follow the energy stream down into the Earth, growing roots from your feet if you feel the need to ground in more.

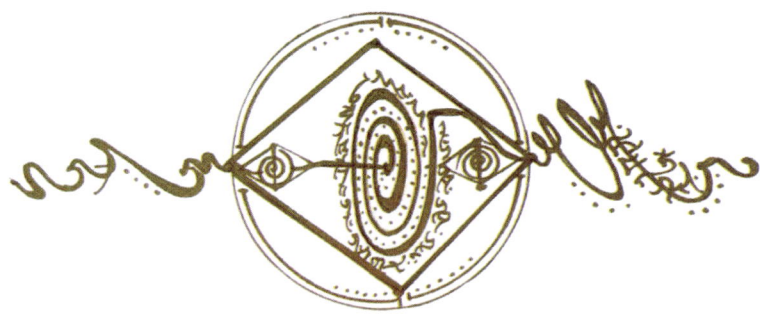

Frequencies to help you move with 5th dimensional currents entering the grids.

"It's time to simplify everything, go back to basics and strip it all away to reveal what you are left with. No distractions, no noise. You are left with clarity, which will help you get to the core of an issue or problem, stripping things back to the bare simple facts of life."

Stromatolite

Pietersite from the mine in Namibia.

Pietersite

Pietersite is an extremely rare stone, only found in Namibia and in Henan Province, China, with colours ranging from deep golds to black, red, blue and clear.

It is a variety of quartz, composed naturally of tiger's eye, hawk's eye and cat's eye quartz. Cat's eye is a wonderful talisman of unwavering protection, distinguished by its special optical phenomena, known as chatoyancy, which is an optical reflectance effect. Its connection to animals is so strong because of the minerals that are in its makeup.

Pietersite Vision

My first exchange with Pietersite was magical, and I will never forget it because it brought the animal guardians to me in full flow. I lay with the Pietersite on my third eye, asking for the ancestors' guidance when the wolves came to me. First came a proud-looking mother wolf on her own out in the forest, and then her pack of cubs. I saw her first, then she jumped into me and I began to shapeshift into her. I stared through her eyes at the forest floor and up at the night sky full of stars. I looked to see my cubs lying sleeping in the leaves and I felt a pang of fear, fear that I could not provide for them, and they were hungry. Then I started to feel my mouth salivate and smelt the cool, crisp air. All of my senses were sharp and alive. I heard a noise in the distance, a twig breaking under foot, and I hunched my head low.

I left my cubs, concerned to leave but knowing we needed food, and I went out hunting. I was an expert hunter and caught a hare quickly. I could feel this life between my teeth and knew I did good; I had provided for my young. In the moment I was surprised at these thoughts and feelings, and that they could be so similar to how I felt about my child. Perhaps that's why the wolf came to me: to show me how connected to all things I am and how we are the same.

The experience with the wolf was complete and I found myself icy cold and in the depths of the North Atlantic Ocean, so far down that all that surrounded me was silence and darkness. It took me a while to adjust to where I was. It fully dawned on me when I was looking through these huge saucer-like eyes that I was a whale: an enormous humpback whale. I felt like a galactic lightship: I could feel the sound pulses echo through the waters as I connected with other beings there. I coasted so effortlessly with grace through the waters on a mission of connection. Suddenly I was back in my body, on Earth.

Pietersite's Medicine

Pietersite is a fast-moving, protective, clearing grandfather energy, which brings the masculine into balance and shakes up the body through emotional and mental layers with an electric charge and a transmuting fire. It is a transformer stone that brings change and new beginnings, grounding the full spectrum of electro-magnetic energy. It is an extremely shamanic stone that will assist you in inter-dimensional travel, vision quests and journeying. It brings the ability to shapeshift and to share the sight of the animal spirits. It has such a primal animal energy to work with and it will bring forward the fires within you, the sharpness of your senses and the rawness of your powers. Its energy likes to move up and expand your higher chakras where it will open and expand your stellar gateway chakra, supporting you to access very high states of altered awareness very quickly.

Its energy is a wise elder energy, who speaks no nonsense, and its role in this course and with the collective now is to create channels for change, including streaming eighth and ninth dimensional light into the lightbody and grids. Look to it to bring up pent-up energy and any internalized feelings to the surface, supporting a held emotional release. Then it moves to link up pathways of light through your body to create more movement and flow around the area that energy took space. Place it on the body where you feel emotions surfacing. It helps to clear stagnant energies, habits and patterns, while revealing new directions for your life and it will support you in bringing action to your goals and make progress moving forward. Pietersite is all about movement too. It activates movement in cells, speeding them up, and it encourages dance and bringing fluidity to the body and limbs to support release.

On the physical side it works on the pituitary gland, balancing the endocrine system and the production of hormones governing the metabolism, blood pressure, libido and body temperature. It supports the chest and breathing. It is a nervous-system stone, stimulating and strengthening the nerves and the brain, helping to ease headaches, stomach pain, dizziness and breathing difficulties as it moves to clear and support the chest and rib cage, and is therefore useful for someone who suffers from panic attacks and anxiety. Thought to ease eye infections, Pietersite is also reported by some users to improve long-distance focus and night vision.

How to Work With Pietersite

Place it on the solar plexus, sacral chakra and/or third eye and it will activate and align their energy channels in union, clearing and connecting their pathways. It grounds the body's physical energy centres, not to the Earth, but to etheric realms. This is a rare gift that increases the focus of your soul's purpose, enhancing visionary and telepathic powers. If you are generally an ungrounded person I would recommend bringing extra grounding stones into your work with it at your root, unless you purposefully seek this out as a focused intent.

When placed on the throat, it will help you speak out and recognize the truth in other's words and actions.

A close-up of Pietersite.

Connect With Pietersite

You will need a piece of Pietersite. If you do not have any you can connect with its energy through the energies of this stromatolite and Pietersite grid on page 198.

★ Hold the intent and state out loud: "I wish to connect with the ancient wisdom you know, through you, your light and the crystalline grids to all pockets of Pietersite in Namibia. I connect fully to the consciousness of Pietersite and its over souls and guardians."

★ Imagine you are holding a piece of Pietersite in your hands as it hears and connects with your words and lights up, bursting in colours. Its rays move through your hands and into your heart, and you allow them to move around your body.

★ You may feel many energies of the guardians come close and you welcome them to you as they circle you. Feel the air whip through your body and energy systems. Feel the fires within you stir on connection with this energy source. Allow Pietersite's energy to collect, move and pool exactly where it wishes to go in your body.

★ When you feel you are connected, with its light energies moving through you, you can ask it: "What is your medicine for me?"

"Take a pause and be more perceptive to your environment and those around you; step back and take a look at what is in ebb and flow. There are a great many and vast things that affect our inner tides. You are stuck in your own inner world and need to look to the cause and effect, the relationship between two events or situations that caused the other. What was the initiating event that brought you to this place, and the effect of that on you and your family, your soul group, and your community? It's important to look at how this situation not only affects you but those around you, and how you can focus on them at this time. To come out of the 'I' and into the 'we' and the 'us'."

Pietersite

A crystal grid to spiral in new energies with
Ammonite, citrine, rose quartz and serpentine.

Ammonite

**When you hold Ammonite, you hold
the knowledge of ancient Earth.**

Ammonites are an extinct group of mollusc animals that date back to 420 million years ago. Because they were alive and well during a very different world than we live in today, they hold records of those ancient energies for us to learn from and connect with. They imbue the energies of strength, longevity and perseverance in to you. It has the soul's path encoded within it, and gazing at the spiral can take you beyond the origins of Earth and into the structure of the universe itself. It will create a special momentum of movement from within and around you, which can be worked with to wind in new, fresh energy and release stagnation. It supports the transformation process of re-birthing yourself, while promoting structure and offering great clarity, especially when you need help uncovering your soul's true path.

The spiral represents connectivity to the divine, and the outer ego (the outside world) into the inner soul (cosmic awareness). It is the evolution and growth of spirit. It is change and development and represents the cycles of life, the peace of coming full circle and knowing a place for the first time. I love to work with the spiral through my grids, especially when I am asked to clear a property of unwanted energies. I create a spiral grid of rosemary and clear quartz at the centre point of the property and bring the property into balance with it. If you want to create change in your life and feel stuck, consider working with the spiral, whether it is gridding around an Ammonite, or creating a spiral creatively like I do on retreats (see photo opposite) with crystal or flowers. It will bring in a flow of energy and clear the way for you. As it brings renewal of fresh energies to you, they spiral into your energy body through all layers, increasing a free and smooth flow of chi throughout the body that spirals around each cell and within each strand of DNA. They are perfect for anyone who is starting on a new project, chapter or stage of life.

As an activating stone of the lower chakras, it speaks to the kundalini and calls it to rise in harmony through you. It also activates life path energies to help you see more clearly and with focus the way you need to go. As well as bringing a flow that activates and the energy bodies through absorbing cosmic energies over eons of time, it is a karmic cleanser, and a very powerful Earth healing tool.

On one of my Glastonbury retreats we created the altar grid together with offerings and home-grown flowers.

Working With Ammonite and the Spiral

Ammonities call in warmth and fire to help you transmute negative and lower vibrations and then warm the energy body up, while helping you bring in higher-vibrational energy from your higher chakras through your crown. I place one on all of my chakras in turn, and as I do, I spiral my hand above it, moving energy through, calling in the light to help my energy field process all the change. It's a great tool to activate personal empowerment.

Place it on the root to improve and increase the flow of life-force energy to bring feelings of safety and groundedness in the body. Connect it consciously with the kundalini flow to activate, and stir it to move, bringing creativity, movement and empowerment.

Creating the spiral with crystals and flowers
to welcome in new energies and change.

Creating a Spiral Crystal Grid
to Welcome in the New

Create a spiral grid to focus newer high-frequency energies into the Earth, a building or space. I often create these when I am cleansing a property of unwanted spirits or lower/dense energies.

You will need crystals, flowers and salt.

* Begin by holding your crystals to your heart to attune them to the invention. Say this out loud or in your head:
* Please support me in clearing this space of all unwanted and lower vibrational energies that seek to disrupt and distract.
* Then choose the start of your spiral, your centre point. I often use a spherical crystal as it radiates energy in all directions, or a flower in full bloom as it mimics the same action. Have fun spiralling outward with flowers and crystal interspersed together. If you have crystal points you want to direct energy around this spiral, so be sure to face the pointed end in the direction the spiral is going.
* Sit with this grid, connecting with the flow of energy through it, and ask to place this with the highest intent within the Earth. I always see the grid sink into the Earth in a bubble of light where its energy and loving intent is distributed through the Earth. The faeries and elementals always love this and find them really fun.
* You can leave this grid out on the land if it feels right; it's a nice reminder of change and cleansing every time you see it.

★ Often in this kind of grid if I am clearing I use crystals such as selenite, clear quartz or clear apophyllite to cleanse and detoxify. Amethyst is useful to add to support transmutation of negative to positive. I also use cleansing and protective herbs such as sage and rosemary woven through.

This spiral was created on the land of a client's property to welcome and ground in the new energies of harmony and balance with selenite, clear quartz and pyrite, after I had cleared the land, space and surroundings.

"Surround yourself with the spiral. I wind in new fresh energies into your body to help move stagnant energy and bring ease of flow. I will convert any negative energy, stagnancy or blockages in your systems by gently flowing in a smooth spiral flow of *chi*, or life-force energy. Visualize my energy swirling around each cell and each strand of DNA. Mine is a gentle karmic cleansing energy to unlock and expand in more light."

Ammonite

Crystal grid created with the intent to activate the
heart and solar plexus to support the release of
past emotions and to reawaken cellular memory.
The heart-shaped stones were collected at the Cave
of the Oracles in Greece, previously mentioned
on page 166. It contains Magnetite with galena
and sphalerite, golden healer tumble stones, raw
emeralds, quartz platonic solids and copper.

Magnetite

Magnetite is a highly magnetic iron oxide rock mineral, which usually forms in octahedral crystals. It's found in high-temperature igneous and metamorphic rocks and in sulfide veins. It is mined as one of the main iron ores on this planet.

Magnetite was originally called "lodestone" as early as 1548, and other names such as magnetic hematite. In 1845 it was given the name Magnetite because natural magnets (lodestones) were known to the ancient Greeks. They called the mineral "Magnet", as it was found in the lands of Magnetes (Magnesia) in Thessaly. There is also a story that it was named after Magnes, a Greek shepherd boy. Magnes noticed that the iron of his staff and the nails on his shoes clung to a Magnetite-bearing rock.

I have always found Magnetite a wonderful addition to crystals grids for calling in what you wish to magnetize to you. It has always sung songs about the Earth grids and its focus to bring polarity balancing (as it has a strong positive-negative polarity), by creating a strong and clear resonance through your energetic field through all layers. It's magnetic therapy that will sit on your body. Its energy is fast moving so it will work on your energy meridians and bio-magnetic field. In essence what that means is this: it wishes to bring you in complete alignment with the Earth's magnetic north and aligns and grounds the lower chakras to Earth's energies. This creates harmony and restores balance on all levels, through the male and female aspects of mind, body and emotions.

Magnetite reminds me a lot of sea coal, with its very intelligent and complex voice and knowledge of the Earth's energies. It has an incredibly busy and sharp energy: it's constantly on the move, working around and through you. It never stops. I often witness it multiply in the lightbody. So often one piece is enough for body work as it re-pins light through the body and reverses any negative currents and programs that may have been running in your energy body that are anchored to any chakra centres.

Magnetite's energy removes energy blockages, renewing and balancing the energy flow and emotions in the aura and lightbody. Offering a healing space for other crystalline energy to dig deeper, it builds the strength and core grounding in the body. In crystal body layouts or healing grids, Magnetite facilitates the flow of energy in the meridians of the physical body and initiates hemispheric balance in the brain, and supports alignment with the etheric body. It holds a strong Sirian energy. The Sirian beings take the mission work seriously and this is what I feel of this stone: it knows its place in the whole and is ready to share with you vast knowledge on the Earth grids and their interconnectivity. It especially likes to work closely with the tree roots and mycelium networks to pass and transmit messages from them.

Many of the ancient giant quartz crystals from Atlantis were moved underground to areas of the Earth with a high quantity of lodestones, because Magnetite can hold their frequencies in a grid of protection, so we can access and find them when humanities consciousness is ready. It will help you recognize dualities that exist around you, and removes old obstacles that have taken root within you, all the while stimulating a fire in your belly to spark confidence and motivation.

We are being asked by the Sirian star councils to do more with the metals alongside crystals and in grids, which includes Magnetite, meteorites, galena and anything with iron in. The metals really add a strong field of grounding to anchor these grids in place where needed. It is a grounding and calming stone, which deepens meditation by just connecting and holding it in your hand, providing a strong grounding cord with the Earth. Energy workers could place them around a client or on the body to instantly pull them back in their body, so to speak, especially after travels and journey work. Its magnetic properties make it a highly effective spiritual grounding stone. Magnetite will tap into events that happen in your life to support a peaceful grounded outlook and approach to healing them, by helping you to release fear, anger and attachment.

Light language to support Magnetite's
energies of clearing and realigning the
energy body through all layers.

Working With Magnetite

Magnetite is a stone that's really keen to be placed on the body to support the grounding of new growth and expansion. It has a gift of bringing balance not only to the meridians and body, but specifically to the hemispheres of the brain, and scientists have even discovered evidence that Magnetite exists in the human brain. It will work on and around the pineal gland to send currents that will revitalize and take away desensitization.

* Place it on your third eye and follow its focused beam of energy into the centre point of your brain as it ripples out its energies to support you. Follow them and observe them.
* Hold or connect with Magnetite's energy and affirm: "I release all burdens old and new, past and present, all expectations, all responsibility, all so I can move forward in light."

Working With Magnetite for Earth Gridding

Place Magnetite in or on the area of disturbed energy to support the healing of the Earth and to support the ley lines. It will establish its vibration and instantly attune to the Earth's electromagnetic field to support realignment, as it does with us and our energy pathways.

Crystals to combine with it in healing work and in a grid are black tourmaline, obsidian, jet and smoky quartz.

Releasing Trapped Pain With Magnetite and the Angels

For this meditation we focus on the wombspace to unlock, disarm and support creation.

You will need a piece of Magnetite, or you can connect with it through the photograph of the Magnetite on page 228.

★ Lie down and place the Magnetite across your womb in a horizontal line. If you do not have a womb, lay it on your abdomen. If you cannot lie down, hold it against your wombspace or abdomen. Or if you do not have a physical piece, call it into your being and visualize it sweeping across your womb or abdomen from left to right.

★ Drop into your heart and your body with your breath and create a chamber of 5D light around you, filling it with a diamond flame that expands through your being.

★ Bring awareness to your wombspace and feel it fully. Place your hands there if you wish, breathe into it and allow your wombspace or abdomen to expand.

★ Bring awareness to the Magnetite resting on your womb. As you do it glows and vibrates quicker, allowing the Magnetite to drop into your expansive womb or abdomen and move its energy exactly to where it needs to be.

★ Invoke the divine director, master cosmos and lords and ladies of light and karma to witness and oversee, as you call in your highest dimensional aspects of light to witness and support in all the ways they can provide, in line with your highest and greatest good.

* A high vibrational angelic pool of white light starts to flow into your space, and a portal starts to open in front of you.
* Allow yourself to float into that light, feeling its warmth, hearing the angels sing and knowing that you are held and supported in so much love.
* You come out the other side into the angelic plane where you are greeted by your angelic team of archangels and seraphim. Feel their love and wings envelop you with light.
* They guide you to a healing pod and once inside they close the entrance.
* You feel your body attune to the high frequency in the space, hearing the angels sing all around you. Their sonics bring peace and relaxation to your body now.
* Ask that the Magnetite and the highest frequencies of the angels locate acute pain in the body.
* You feel and see the Magnetite moving through you to identify ancient stored pain. It will be in many places at once, multiplying, as it locks that pain in its energy field to dissolve it.
* This ancient pain is given a space now to be seen and heard. What is this pain? Whose is this pain? Call forward those who have shared this pain to come close to the pod to receive healing through the beautiful threads of life that connect us.
* Healing source light is rippling from above and below, through all threads that connect you and these parts of you to your ancestors and other star beings.
* Ask Magnetite to seek out the root core of this pain and trace back through all entanglements, any cords, threads of disharmony in your field, back to the planet and being of origin.

★ Freeze this dissident thread, cord or connection and shatter it. It is no more. In the light are the truth and love of mother and father god.

★ All beings and parts of you that were entangled let out a cry of release as they are freed from this entanglement, all the way back to planet and or being of origin. You feel or see them all release.

Magnetite octahedral crystals.

"I provide a highly effective spiritual grounding cord into the Earth, activating all chakras and aligning you with the Earth's chakras. Call on me to fill your root with an abundance of Earth energy. I wish to provide you with a full-bodied, balanced, grounded energy to support expansion in all areas of your life."

Magnetite

Close up of Vanadinite.

Vanadinite

Vanadinite is a rare member of the apatite family, combining lead, vanadium, oxygen and chlorine. Its structure is very unusual as it contains neutrons that hold valence electrons. They have the unique ability to absorb certain wavelengths of colour in the visible light spectrum, so that when light enters the crystal's surface, these electrons cause the red colour to be present.

It's so interesting that it absorbs colour rays through its very makeup. I felt there is more to this from a metaphysical (energy) point of view and of course I asked the stone. It shows me that each hexagonal crystal has the potential to hold a spectrum of rainbow of light of a very high-frequency, absorbing and keeping it for you to enhance your energy work. She says that she has so much more hidden within. A sentiment that could be said of you too. If you take your energy inside one of her orange hexagonal chambers you receive many rays of light to recharge you. She shows us a chameleon: it changes colour to adapt to its environment, and as it begins to walk away, it flashes streaks of light and colour, which make it stand out like a bolt of lightning, lighting the way.

Vanadinite will really stir something beautiful within you. She will help boost and stir your inner fires of creativity so you can express what is in your heart, whether it's through colour and art, writing and movement. She tells me that her role is the "muse". She inspires, but only inspires. She is very clear on that: you must nurture and birth the ideas.

Vanadinite offers us another beautiful image of young women dancing and singing in a circle, invoking sisterhood and community. She is very much connected to goddess energy, and particularly the aspect of the triple goddess, the Maiden, bringing the wisdom and lightness of all qualities of the Maiden aspect: dawn and sunset, the season of spring, the energies of youth, innocence, self-confidence, independence, growth. This is the crescent-to-waxing phase of the moon. She represents beauty, potential and new life, and encourages you to express yourself, and to explore and discover. Her guardian goddess energy are the three Graces, who dance around her. They are the three daughters of Zeus and Hera. Aglaia (Brightness) Euphrosyne (Joyfulness) and Thalia (Bloom). The connection to ancient Greece for past life viewing and connection is strong in this stone.

This stone spires a real fire in your sacral chakra and wombspace. It will stimulate and wake up sexual energy in a powerful way, connecting you to primal animal energies that may have been hidden or locked away, bringing passion to all you do. Placing Vanadinite under your pillow will help you wake up feeling energized. It will also bring order to your thoughts. If you are feeling confused or scattered, having it close will help.

As I held Vanadinite, connecting with her flow, she asked me to dig deeper and look into when she was first found by

Western science, which was in Purisma del Cardonel mine, near Zimapan, Mexico, in 1801. Its compound was then investigated, as it was suspected of containing a new element. A mineral researcher named Nils Gabriel Sefstrom was able to isolate the hidden metal element, "erythronium". Sefstrom named the new element vanadium after Vanadis, Norse goddess of love and beauty. Vanadis is also known as Freyja/Freya. In the rituals of the triple goddess it is Freya, the Norse goddess who represents the maiden aspect of the goddess (as well as Rhiannon, Persephone and Artemis). I find it interesting what people name crystals upon finding them as I feel the divine working through them to often give us a hint of connection and meaning through the stone.

On the physical layer Vanadinite is considered to be good for respiration and tosupport circulation of oxygen in the lungs.

Creating a crystal grid with Vanadinite, rose quartz and red jasper around an iron-rich crystal skull.

Working With Vanadinite

It is important to note that Vanadinite is fragile, so when cleansing it keep it out of water, and just cleanse with visualization, sound, herbs and lunar energy, and charge with solar energy.

Do not use it to make elixirs, as it is a mix of elementals and can be known to be toxic to ingest. If making a crystal elixir please use the indirect method. This involves placing the crystal close to or onto the container to infuse it directly with its energy. It is not added to the fluid.

If you do not have any Vanadinite please take the time before to connect with the photograph on page 234 before this activation.

You will need a piece of Vanadinite.

★ Vanadinite connects strongly with the third eye, sacral, base and earth star chakras.

★ Place a piece below your feet in the area of your earth star chakra. It will bring energy down through you to your earth star to help you ground yourself physically, helping you go about tasks in a more practical way. It is a strong grounding stone, and using it in meditation will help you come out of it not feeling spaced out.

★ Work with it at your sacral and root chakras to bring focus. It will organize and focus your thoughts around manifesting your desire, helping you bridge your goals to the Earth realm, bringing that idea back down to Mother Earth to be nurtured.

Connecting to the Womb With Vanadinite

This journey is to get you into the womb and enhance connection and creativity.

You will need a piece of Vanadinite. If you do not have any, take the time before to connect with the photograph before this activation. Use a journal and pen to make any notes of feelings it brings up.

★ Take your time to sit down comfortably. Sit up, noticing how elongated and straight your spine is, with your heart open.

★ Think of someone who you unconditionally love and feel that love radiating through you as a pink ray. As your heart opens up to the love you feel it opens front and back above and below, shining out the brightest light. Now rub your hands together to activate the loving flow through them.

★ Place both hands on your womb, wherever it feels comfortable to you. And when you place them there feel a connection of light from your hands flowing into your womb.

★ There's a beautiful flow of love from your heart into your womb like a river, as you see a pink, gold and silver bridge of light forming from your heart, descending down to your womb. This consciously connects the heart and womb fully through all planes, dimensions and existence, to the cosmic heart, Venus and all planetary heart unity grids.

★ Tune in to your womb by breathing. Focus into it three times, with long, slow breaths as these pink waters continue to flow through you. Be in your womb; feel her heartbeat and her songs.

★ Now you are in your womb, connected and flowing with unconditional love. I would love for you to sit in the centre of your womb, allowing it to unfold for you however it wishes to appear. When sitting in your womb I want you to ask your womb how it feels and take note of any words that come, and feelings, emotions or even colours. Write them down if you feel you want to.

★ Now you are in your womb, call in the energies of Vanadinite. Paint it into being and see it appear in the centre of your womb. Here it glows orange and golden, intensifying and expanding with each breath. It begins to spin faster and faster as its fires radiate through your womb and warm it up. Let it know that you are about to go on a journey with it, to release, expand and open to its majesty.

★ As you sit in your womb you get a glimpse of its mystery as a cosmic portal shows itself at the back of your wombspace. You see far off galaxies and stars inviting you in. This is the potential to create and connect that we are unlocking in this course.

★ Open your eyes and come back to this moment.

Close up of Vanadinite.

"This is the chameleon's survival mechanism, to camouflage to survive. You have been asked to do that and you have done as well as you can fitting into a society with structures that are crumbling. I am here to tell you that this is shifting. You are the way-showers of this higher-frequency shift on this Earth, and now it's not the time to blend in or to camouflage. This is the time to show all facets of yourself, your colour and light. And I am here to help you bring forward creative change and action through you."

Vanadinite

Cintamani stones grid around a lava stone skull.

Tektites

It felt important to talk about Tektites in this book as we explore Earth's ancestors and guardians. This extends to our star ancestors too. In layman's terms, Tektites are terrestrial debris created and ejected during meteorite impacts.

Made up of natural glass formed from extreme pressure and heat, my favourite for so long was Moldavite, a Pleiadian connector, and a heart-centred cosmic traveller with the ability to take you up so high. I always work with strong grounding stones alongside it to make sure I make it back down!

 ## Moldavite

It's been some time since I picked it up. The energy had gone into hibernation until recently; it had had a new surge through the crystalline grid of information transmitting through it. You find this with the Tektites: they can often sleep, then wake up.

There was a painter in my house who noticed my crystals and asked me about what I do. He confessed his love of stone circles and dragons, and that he had no one to talk to about it, which led to the most beautiful talk about the universe.

The next day we spoke again and as we did I saw an aspect of him come in from Alpha Centauri, so I spoke his star frequency to him instead of words. His face was a picture: he looked so happy, he closed his eyes and smiled. I let it sink in and it led to some impromptu energy work (my favourite kind) in my kitchen.

When he left I felt the need to give him a piece of Moldavite to work with on his third eye. Guiding him in how to receive its green ray and the ways it wanted to merge with his lightbody, I warned him that it would take him very high, and very fast. He was ready. As I held it and attuned it, three energies from his star set came in ready to take him travelling. I saw this star ship but didn't tell him, as I didn't want to affect his experience. I asked him to release expectations as much as he could and to just flow without attaching. The next morning he came in all excited and told me the stone had shown him so much geometry and a huge ball of light entered his space, which he merged with and it shot him off to a part of the universe that shined pink and green like an aurora borealis. He said it was so fast it made him a bit dizzy when he came back around. "You went in a ship! I knew it!" I screeched, a bit too excited, but I could feel what was opening up for him. I armed him with some black tourmaline for his next travels to balance him a bit and to anchor him. He left and I never saw him again, but the exchange is etched in my memory. Life is magical and these exchanges of love and connection are what I live for. I am so grateful for the incredible people the stones bring into my life, each one divinely orchestrated, never a coincidence.

A personal piece of Moldavite that works with people
to connect them directly to their star family.

Golden Libyan Desert Glass

Golden Libyan Desert Glass is found strewn across the desert between Libya and Egypt. It is said to be older than Moldavite, and was formed when an asteroid hit the Earth about 29 million years ago, making it about 14 million years older. It will detect disharmony in your field and cosmic entanglements that do not serve you and freeze them, then shatter them safely to be recycled in source light. This clears the disharmony through all fields and dimensions and beyond the 3D time. It will awaken the Sirian light codes within you and your connection and work through that star set. Many people link the stone to Orion. It will enhance and lift sacred geometry templates held in your field, and the journey it wishes to take you on is one of expansion through your soul's keys and cosmic mastery. It is a stone of illumination, and transmits the golden ray, which

Golden Libyan Desert Glass.

is thought of as one of the highest vibrations of light the body can receive.

A key mission by the over-lighting guardians is to reinstate your harmonic DNA, to bring back tones to you that have been taken or manipulated through your lives. When connected with it fully, placing it on the higher heart blasts a wave of sound through the heart connecting through you and all of your higher vibrational aspects, to clear through all fields and dimensions and beyond the 3D time matrix. This speaks volumes as to what a potent healing tool it is to unify the parts we are collecting back and reconnecting with. All versions of you connect through the golden wave created in your heart. This happens instantaneously. You might find that it takes time to connect with Golden Libyan Desert Glass fully, as it does hold back, and working with it is almost like an initiation of trust in itself, but the guardian energies of this stone ask you to surrender and trust them to guide you

It is a stone that needs to be activated, so I often chant "RA" for 5 to 10 minutes while holding it to my heart with the intent to journey with it and this will activate it. Its energy will respond to sound and pure intentions.

Cintamani Stones

A few years ago a friend visited me to buy some Lemurian crystals, and he came with a collection of high-vibrational crystals he wanted me to take a look at. One of these stones was Cintamani Stone, and he told me that it had been gifted to him by a guardian of that frequency. I had never heard of them or even seen them before. It looked very unassuming, as they are Tektites in glassy brown/black colour with moon-like craters on the surface. As I held it I had a full-body reaction, with shaking hands, and explosions of the cosmos appeared in my light field. I felt the exchange of energies, through their guardians, respecting and bestowing this stone that supports its power. That day I said to the universe that if it sees fit I would love to be a guardian of this stone.

Fast forward to a couple of years later and an email landed in my inbox from a mysterious gentleman called Pat, a light worker form the USA who had picked up these stones in Arizona. It seems the universe answered my call in divine timing, as he said that the goddess had guided him to me to be a guardian of this stone and he would like to send me one. He informed me with passion and wisdom of their origins from Sirius, as a Tektite glass from the cosmos, that there is a huge Cintamani grid in the Earth and waters that has been set by many light workers across the globe, each point plotted by exact location, as there are pieces of Cintamani all over the world. They radiate an energy vortex of rainbow light spanning 20 to 25 kilometres (12.5 to 15.5 miles) when planted in the Earth or water, which brings so much change and support to the grids as well as boundaries against negative and unwanted energies.

I have specifically been working with them to remove high-level implants in lightworkers that stop them from reaching higher than the seventh-dimensional level consciously. They serve and communicate with dragon grids and the many mountains of the world, which are galactic hubs of energies coming in and out. I have built a beautiful relationship with this

Golden energies of unity.

fellow light worker who offered to provide me with the stones
as a guardian to send out to others I see fit to work with and
protect them in light. When I received my piece from Pat I
went to my garden to sit under my ash tree and I drummed in

celebration to welcome it to my land. As I held it up to the sun it glowed and connected with the Earth grids on my land. This is something I do with all stones that find me.

The myth of Cintamani is found throughout Hindu and Buddhist cultures. It is widespread through China, Mongolia and other cultures from southeast Asia, similar to the stories of the philosopher's stone in the western world. The legend around Cintamani in Buddhism is that it is one of four relics that came in a chest that fell from the sky, during the reign of King Lha Thothori Nyantsen of Tibet, China. The king did not understand their purpose but kept them respected and with reverence.

It is said to represent a stone that can fulfil wishes. Pat collects these pieces from his home in Arizona and sends them to me. Some people have given these Tektites the name of Saffordites (or Arizona Tektites) and would suggest they are members of the obsidian glass family. I really don't care what they are called as it's more about the vibration they carry, the way they make you feel and your experience with them, as many crystals get given so many nicknames that it gets confusing. For this chapter I choose to call them what I know them to be, Cintamani Stones, because they bring so much Sirian light and solar codes through Helios. They synthesize vibrations into love, light and grace. The most common reference is that they are a gift to Earth from the sky, and evidence proves that this stone came from the Sirius star system some millions of years ago. It happened during a galactic super wave when a planet that was orbiting Sirius A exploded and flew in all directions, and some of the fragments reached Earth. They began revealing themselves recently in 2014, to assist us on the ascension path to a golden age. So it's more important than ever to learn and work with this stone's energy. It is a stone with the highest vibration of all stones known, said to be even more powerful than Moldavite, but working with them together creates a beautiful union.

I have known them to awaken you to galactic missions, a pure light strengthening inner guidance and connection to your highest self.

Creating Golden Sphere Vacuums

If you have the chance to hold a piece of Tektite in your hand you will find it creates energetic surges of light that create powerful golden spheres for healing. They are a vacuum for energy, for light or dark. This is the choice of the user. It's important that we always work with crystals with the purest intention. These spheres can be harnessed through many dimensions and multiplied in form to hold and lock sonic energy for sonic resonance healing: a quantum healing principle used and shared during the time of Atlantis

Golden Libyan Desert Glass is rare, which makes it expensive, so if you do not have any you can take some time to connect through the photograph provided on page 246 while saying:

"I open up my heart to connect with your wisdom and guidance. I am ready to hear, see and feel all that is in alignment with my highest good."

You will need Golden Libyan Desert Glass – or you can call its energy through you from the photograph.

* Imagine you have a piece of this stone in your hand and it starts to glow. Its light starts to form a golden sphere around it. This is a vacuum of sound and light

* As you notice it forming in a complete golden sphere in your hand, it begins to vibrate. This golden sphere of light is for you to place on your body.

* Move your hand toward your body intuitively, as this is where this healing sphere of light and sound wants to go.

* The sphere passes into your body and travels through, multiplying. Each golden sphere locates and identifies distortion (lower or dense fear vibrations in the body) and locks around them.

* You witness as they freeze, shatter and collapse the lower densities they locked within them. You hear the sounds and colours erupt like rainbows from your body as it all falls away from you.

* Breathe in peace.

* Breathe out, releasing any final residual energies, letting it all go.

* Re-ground yourself with water, and go outside to let any excess energies this stirred up within you to run into the Earth to be transmuted. Gaia is always of service to us.

* Express your gratitude to the Earth, your body and this moment.

"I dissolve the illusions Earth can present through systems that were put in place to control. I dissolve the veil of amnesia and connect you to your infinite source power. I dissolve the network of implants and I support divine expression of freedom."

Tektites

Water energies and Lemurian Quartz to help you
in connecting to the golden age of Lemuria.

Lemurian

Lemuria was a golden age that existed approximately 14,000 years ago. It is believed that Lemuria itself existed where the Pacific Ocean and potentially the Indian Ocean are now. There was no fear in Lemuria, no lower vibrations, and their love and high-vibrational essence carried through them, and this vibration merged the waters and all elemental and elemental beings.

In Lemuria, the focus was on creating, living and loving in harmony with nature and the plants. Vast libraries of flower essences and dews were collected and a system of recording started with the cosmic plants for future generations to tune in to. There were stones kept for their beauty and to enhance vibrations: soft rainbow fluorites, soft pink calcites and rose quartz, all very gentle and heart harmonizing, with tones of diamond, pink and peach to amplify those divine rays of love and femininity, being worked into the temples. But mostly quartz that was used to build Lemurian temples, and these held and amplified energies for the lands and waters. The temples were so high vibrational they sang.

Our ancestors knew the importance of crystals as sacred vibrational tools that support our connection to the highest realms of light and consciousness. They knew that all living things were connected through the crystalline grid networks through the planet. Many of us hold cellular memories from the root races spanning Earth's history and many of us have had lives in Lemuria and Atlantis. We know that crystals generated fields of energy around the land and in the waters, creating grid networks that held the field of all creation. The knowledge of this was carried over many other ancient cultures after the fall of Atlantis as many tried to save the teachings and protect the knowledge.

In Lemuria we were not of 3D bodies, so we still had a lot of power over our form, moving molecules to create and shapeshift; we were diamond light traveling through and coming into form, and in our heart was a diamond-seed crystal that we created from. We would harness the energies of the sunlight and the waters in the heart to create and send healing light to where it was needed in the Earth grids. Gathering in circles, many temple elders and adepts would work with the light in their hearts to co-create these beings of light.

There are places that still hold the frequency of Lemuria today, including Sedona, Hawaii, the South Pacific Islands, Easter Island, Fiji, New Zealand, Asia, Australia and into the Indian Oceans. When Lemuria flooded, some of its frequency went into the ocean and shapeshifted into whales, dolphins and mermaids. Other parts went underground into tunnels deep in the Earth to form underground civilizations, for example Mount Shasta in the USA, and there is also a Lemurian base under the island of the sun, in Lake Titicaca, Bolivia, which is the focus of the silver feminine ray on this planet. The Pleiadians were very much a main star race that seeded Lemuria, and they were heart-based teachers with a vast amount of knowledge about crystals.

My heart is bursting with love already at the opportunity to introduce you to the Lemurian energies through this chapter. Everything I am writing about comes from a deep inner knowledge woven with visions of my past lives where I was devoted to the temple of the mother. Here I was a water priestess, shapeshifting and holding consciousness with the whales and dolphins, and creatrix of crystals grids, and the wisdom of Lemuria is one of the divine mother, remembering her creative powers and love. All of my work on this plane now leads back to Lemuria, and awakening the priestess and the sacred knowledge of plants and crystal alchemy. I also love that I chose to incarnate into one of the last matrilineal lines on the Earth.

The Water Priestess of Lemuria and the Crystals in the Water

Lemuria was a pure paradise lived closely with the waters: its people understood all beings of the waters, seas, rivers, waterfalls and lakes. The waters were living, life giving, cleansing, a part of all, and the waterfalls revealed interstellar dimensions and portals to other realms that were travelled through regularly. It was paradise on Earth, with many magical beings in existence in one place living in harmony, including the unicorns, dragons and many elementals.

It was a regular practice to gather in a circle and sing to the water, which was alive as the land was. As we know crystals record and store information, it is important at this time to speak with and listen to the waters and work with their crystal fractals and crystals to bring awakening to cellular memory.

Lemurians could connect with the crystals in the water and bend and mould and restructure them to form shapes. They interacted with the water through their whole, so that its crystals restructured. They could pause the flow of rivers just by talking to the water, and they could move and change the course of rivers and streams if needed, but of course they trusted the innate knowledge of the Earth and its flow. You may have heard the story in the Bible about Moses parting the Red Sea: this has Lemurian origins and some would consider it Atlantean technology. But it is far older, and was an understanding of alchemical alchemy passed down before Atlantis. It was not just a practice or technology, but a deep connection and understanding of crystals and the way the waters are a cosmic conductor for light essence.

Unification Stones

The Lemurians were masters and experts of encoding crystals and bringing the light through the crystals of the Earth. I have a champagne-coloured Lemurian Crystal that is encoded with such a joy frequency that when I found it I couldn't stop giggling and laughing (in photograph opposite). It's important to regularly show these Lemurian Crystals the sun to let the natural light shine through them as they stir cellular memory within you.

Light language activation: golden unification
energies of Lemurian Quartz.

The Lemurians had a diamond-seed crystal in their higher heart, which they created the Lemurian Crystals with. Because they themselves were crystalline they could co-create a crystal vessel with ease, and could use it to hold their consciousness and wisdom. They solidified their light and created the Lemurian Crystals. When creating a crystal sometimes they came together as a group on dates that aligned with important astrological solar moments, when the sun was highest in the sky (the summer months) or during high solar flares, as this was a beneficial time to create. The power of the sun could effortlessly balance the waters that they moved with. Sometimes it would be one priestess that encoded, or sometimes many would include their consciousness at once, depending on the mission and intent at that time.

They left these amazing gifts within the Earth for us, and they were positioned to heal and support the planet and grid systems. They created the first Lemurian seed crystals by anchoring their heart through the crystal core of the Earth. Each stone deeply resonates with Gaia's crystal, bringing up its crystalline light through them, and alchemizing in through the heart with the waters. This liquid light then moved through their crystal seed heart and took form in their hands. I have observed the crystal forming through their being through the process of alchemy, and the golden geometric coding that moved from hearts to surround the forming crystal as it solidified. They could materialize and dematerialize physical objects with ease.

When they had created the crystals they then dedicated them to the Earth and placed them in chambers under the ground to settle. This process was important and could take time. They were grouped together and they shared consciousness, each lighting up as it received information, still connected to the Lemurians that created them, so each elder was able to send a continual stream to them. Like the record keepers of Atlantis, many of them kept the records of the healing frequency of Lemuria. As there was more of a re-calibration through the newly seeded Lemurian seed grid, they worked with the Earth more and more to bring high-frequency pockets to quartz up to the surface for them to work with. They sped up the process of creation of quartz formations by working with the water and Earth so were able to attune a high number of crystals to be distributed through the Earth in specific pockets.

Many groups of Lemurians used the underground tunnel systems to move their crystals. Some went with the civilization as it moved factions to live in underground cities of light, notably in Mount Shasta, USA, Hawaii, the Kauai Gateway, Peru/Bolivia, Lake Titicaca and certain sports in Sedona, USA. There is a portal link to these civilizations at Glastonbury Tor, in the UK, and of course there are more that cannot be named at this time. These are places that hold much wisdom and light of the divine mother, and Mother and Sovereign queen codes of awakening. By visiting these sites you will connect with her energy.

Earth is a living light library of this universe, and there are many libraries within the Earth, from the plant and seed libraries on the inner Earth. The Earth provides many rocks and minerals that can be found nowhere else in the solar system that are of much value to others. The Lemurian star mothers share that their library was the water, and the plants of Lemuria.

To connect with certain bodies of water around the world of Lemurian frequency is to assess their libraries of energies, encoded through the crystal fractals in the water. Here is where all their wisdom lives and it takes certain individuals of specific lineages like us to be able to explore that. The Lemurians worked with all sea creatures. The dolphins were encoded with joy and love and fed that through the waters, the white whales were vast portals of mother energy that doubled up as galactic ships coming through the Andromedan gate to hold tri-frequencies (trinity frequencies) for the unity grids.

Gridding with Lemurian Quartz, on the eclipse in the Yucatan to anchor the divine frequencies of love.

Ascended dolphin beings of a Pleiadian descent and whales of Andromeda offered much support to the seeding of the first crystalline templates in the waters of this Earth in Lemuria. They had the resonance, sound and frequency to carry them deep within the depths, to the lower points of Earth such as the Mariana Trench and many other trenches that have not been uncovered. They worked with the whale mothers to carry light to the depths of the darkness and assisted the planet as well as the Lemurian to get the light out far and wide. The ability to shapeshift goes back to the Lyrans, the original ancestors of this universe. These cat people could shapeshift and those of Lyran-Pleiadian descent brought to Lemuria through their DNA.

The Lemurians were master frequency keepers: they worked closely with planetary frequencies and universal oneness, to encode these crystals the expansive golden geometric coding that would expand and enhance their potential to be conductors.

The use of the electro-magnetic frequencies of the Earth were harnessed in this beautiful process through the Lemurian Crystals, and each crystal resonated with a pole and axatonial flow line within the Earth, so that they knew exactly where to place them in the grids to support harmony through the poles. This is important to know because Lemurian Crystals can bring our body into magnetic alignment with the Earth. If you think of a compass that aligns to magnetic north, this is how the Lemurian Crystals work: they realign and resensitize your body's subtle energy nodes back into harmonic resonance with the Earth. This was the beginning of the technical information streams that supported the Atlantean crystalline technology. The Lemurian Crystals seeded the crystalline grid with the framework and templates for the Atlantean sun crystal grid, setting the scene for much spiritual technology to flow in and through. This wisdom was reserved by the elder mothers of the community, and they passed down this alchemy of the elements through the first mystery schools of cosmic wisdom established by Mother Mary in Lemuria.

As the Lemurians were alchemists and understood the elements they brought in a balance and a harmony through these stones. It was pure alchemy, and we often refer to alchemy as turning base metal to gold, but this was alchemy of balancing the elements with the unified frequency of the mother and father in the higher heart, which the Lemurians did effortlessly because they were unified. Once they created these stones, they brought focus to the Earth's crystalline grid templates. Because they were the creators of this grid template, they connected these Lemurian Crystals. So that the memory and encoded information in them could move and travel through this grid into many other Lemurian stones. It was their inner knowing and the cosmic waters that communicated to them to create these liquid light crystals, combining their heart consciousness and the pure cosmic vibrations of the waters. They understood the place and need for crystal, not for themselves but for us, in the future.

Many pockets of the first Lemurian Crystals were found in the Minas Gerais region of Brazil in 1999. They were called Lemurian seed crystals because they were found unattached to clusters, with a frosty matte finish with horizontal barcoding (laddering) on one or more facets. Geologically they are an anomaly of nature as they represent all formations: channeller, transmitter, manifestation, Isis, twin, dolphin, bridge, phantom, record keeper, enhydro and many more. They have since been found in South Africa, Australia, Madagascar, Columbia and Diamantina in Brazil. It is my understanding that from 2024 a new next wave of unity consciousness will be felt through these stones as more are found, with Australia and Africa being hot spots.

Lemurian Crystals are ascension keys of light, like all quartz, but they have a specific mission to open and activate deeper chambers of the heart. They are a higher vibration of quartz that were carried to many points of the world and hidden for when humanity is ready. We are moving into a time when more Lemurian Quartz of a refined frequency will be found from 2024, as there is a passing of new light that has been recorded for this time and the Lemurians will come from new lands. Lemurian Crystals have been known to be identified through the laddering barcode pattern on one or many facets, which has caused controversy in the metaphysical field as they say that it's just grown formation/patterns on the crystal.

I have not experienced through their creation this being an important part of the process, perhaps at the beginning when humanity was ready to receive their consciousness they had laddering as a focus point to access the energies of the crystal, but consider now as we shift and awaken faster, this laddering is not necessarily something that identifies a Lemurian Crystal: what identifies it is its tender mothering heart energy, and they feel very different from clear quartz, which feels more masculine.

We're moving toward a place of understanding where the laddering is not the integral part of a Lemurian Crystal that identifies it. We need to be as they teach, feeling their teachings in the heart. Many Lemurian Crystals coming out of the ground in the specific areas of Brazil where they were found have little or no laddering, but still hold a very strong Lemurian mother energy.

So how can we identify a quartz as a Lemurian energy? The area it comes from is important: a lot of Lemurian Crystals come from the Minas Gerais region of Brazil. For example, in Corinto, a unique form of quartz called the Code Keeper of Freedom is coming to the surface. It is also known as the Root of Lemuria because it is the quartz's bed of which the Lemurians grow from. This also does not have laddering, and its surface is full of etching, coding and hexagonal keys, where the Lemurian Crystals grow from. I have had the pleasure of working with these stones and they are a journey stone with many keys that take you within the Earth, within your heart and to the deepest parts of you.

 ## The Medicine of Lemurian Quartz

Lemurian Quartz is a heart stone of elevating proportions, reminding you of the beauty, grace and love within you. She does this by lighting up and opening hidden heart chambers and connecting the heart to the higher heart complex. She also brings currents through your highest galactic chakras down to merge into your heart, fostering a strong connection to oneness and the universal heart and mind. She is liquid love, and a pure light, a beacon that radiates the golden energies of Lemuria and the diamond frequencies of the 5D heart.

When I first committed to this journey of awakening in my late twenties I had very clear visions and feeling that I had been a crystal in Lemuria. I saw visions of a giant stone the size

of a house on the land there.
It radiated and transmitted
light for the diamond sun
grids above the Earth, and
I saw myself touch it with
my hands and third eye and
merge into it. I remember
the visceral feeling of liquid
light running through my
body as I became that light
stream. It doesn't matter if
I was the crystal or if I held
consciousness with it. It was
a moving experience that
helped me understand these
crystals to a deep level. Since
then, so many large Lemurian
Crystals find me for me to
pass them on.

I'm passionate about
Lemurians from Brazil,
because something about the
land's energies feel familiar. I
have many Lemurian Crystals
that come with me across
the world to sacred sites,
and I grid them as I find their
vibration such pure carriers
of light. A few years ago a

Gridding in the Yucatán,
Mexico, with my
champagne Lemurian,
which comes with
me everywhere.

Brazilian crystal miner found me. Marcello was a wizard so in tune and connected to the alchemy of the Earth. He had a direct relationship with the mining community in Minas Gerais and mined himself, and he also tried to educate other families on how to open up veins on their land and collect them safely and with respect. I started to buy my Lemurian Crystals from him. He had opened a vein in his land and his family were on hand to clean and pack the stones for me. He would often send me photographs of the plants, flowers and waters on the land that the crystal came from around the dig site so I could connect with the area. I loved the fact I had formed this close connection to this elemental soul, and I loved that I knew exactly who had collected and touched my crystals every step of the way, and that they had preserved them with respect in dedication to the Earth. Not many crystal sellers can tell you exactly who has picked your stones from the Earth as they get passed through many people.

There is a direct link to Lemurian Crystals and the waters, as they were formed in and with the water's consciousness and when we work with the waters and clear the waterways of the world we re-activate more golden age Lemurian wisdom. The water being feminine, these stones nurture the feminine within you.

If you have a Lemurian Crystal, always take it to the water and place it in water to connect and send its light, and something quite magical will happen. I was at Stonehenge recently and the sarsen stones were singing, if a little quietly. It started to rain and they told me that they love the rain that their vibration lifts in the rain and they sing with more gusto. So water does really add to all of the stones' energy and this is why we are advised to cleanse certain crystals in water.

Working With Lemurian Quartz's Medicine

★ When working with the Lemurian frequency, it is important to connect and invoke the pure crystalline waters of the Pleiades to flow through you. Visualize it pouring down from the Seven Sisters star constellation like a waterfall, entering and energizing your body and heart as you call your Lemurian Crystal into your heart to open. Connecting with the waters and the sea creatures is key to opening a Lemurian Crystal's wisdom.

★ Activating crystals with sound: the priestess taught that when connecting with crystals you should chant, holding them to your heart. In Atlantis they did not have to activate the crystals as they were fully awake, since these were times we were so connected to source and oneness. As humanity has closed off more from the source the ways we work with crystals have limited greatly, now we are opening up and blossoming the crystals are responding and new crystals are making themselves known as we are ready.

★ The aquamarine ray is the ray of the mother, and a ray that was conducted through the waters. It was focused in the temple of the mother, which housed the aquamarine flame with the white diamond core which you will find in the base of your spine. To connect with this energy you can work with a Lemurian Crystal or place aquamarine, diamond and pearl on your heart.

A reminder to be open to the magic and wonder around you and under your feet. This photo was taken of Lara at a diamond grid work gathering in Sedona, Arizona. Caitlin captured Lara's beautiful rainbow soul perfectly as we tuned in to this frequency.

Lemurian Quartz Journey

You will need a Lemurian Quartz, or to gaze at my Lemurian Crystal in the photograph on the cover of this book. If you wish to make it more potent and have some quartz, arrange them in a circle and sit in the centre of it (points facing inward toward you).

★ If you have a Lemurian Crystal, take it in your hand now and drop into your heart's flame. When the magic, mystery and alchemy happens, take three breaths, holding the intent to connect with the core of this Lemurian light in your hands.

★ Now breathe in and feel it glow in your hands on connection, getting brighter with each breath.

★ Call in the over-lighting energies of Lemuria to hold you now in a sphere of diamond light.

★ Ask that the Pleiadian council of light that supported the seeding of the Lemurian Crystals into the grid come forward to surround you in a sphere of their light

★ As they do the crystal starts to come to life in your hands, and golden geometry and coding appear, flashing through its aura.

★ Observe and witness the wonder, thanking the star guides and ancestors for their potent energies of remembrance.

★ Hold that crystal to your heart close and breathe in its golden glow, absorbing all geometry as it flows into your heart, body, organs, bones, cells and waters.

★ Take your time feeling, breathing its energy, connecting with the guides and receiving anything they wish to offer you.

★ Paint the picture around you of a lush tropical paradise, peppered with deep green fern plants and bright red hibiscus flowers. In the distance you hear the sparkle of water and see a waterfall through the palm trees. You transport yourself to Lemuria, where the Earth glistens with rainbow hues, and every part of nature around you sings and moves in joy. You are in heaven on Earth: truly the garden of paradise we often read about.

★ We now hold this vision and our feelings of love for golden Lemuria together.

★ Take a few breaths of this glorious energy around you. It enters your body like treacle, nurturing and warm; it is home.

★ Let the energies of the crystal flow into your hands, body and heart like water, not attaching but just observing where it flows and what it lights up within you.

Lemurian Quartz gridded on an amplifying light-coded base.

Unity Consciousness

Remember that YOU are the crystal and the crystalline vessel that is moving humanity forward.

Connecting with crystals is all about being and connecting with the heart.

A pure heart vibration of love is the most important spiritual component to receive. It transmits omnipresent directional forces of love, and from being in that space, cellular knowing arises. It is this space you are moving toward or entering into now, the sacred heart resonance field.

Triangle record keeper markings on my starberry quartz.

Being in the deepest chamber of the heart holds the feeling and language that communicates directly with the source. It gives us the gift of unconditional love and peace. When we recognize that signature we can feel with greater awareness, by holding the light and staying neutral and in love.

I could not end this book without mentioning quartz,

which is the most abundant stone on this Earth. I have a clear quartz point that travels everywhere with me, recording all of the energy interactions, in ceremony and through the grids.

It comes with me to amplify and conduct energies, which quartz is very good at. In Atlantis, giant clear quartz record keeper crystals were situated in all the temples, and they did this exact job: conducting, amplifying, enhancing and recording. It is my favourite stone. As I sat with it, like I often do, I asked it to tell me a story, and it said: "No, you tell me yours."

I felt this was the perfect ending, even though we know the journey never ends. My clear quartz's consciousness summed up precisely what we must do: we must continue to listen and pass on the stories of the land of our ancestors, of the stones.

Meditation on cathedral rock with my
Lemurian Quartz, which travels with me.

"My song is one of joy,

The simple joy of pure presence.

Did you know the joy elevates as
laughter does; it comes hand in hand.

When you flow with joy you see
everything with fresh new eyes.

The mundane becomes magical,

Because you find new angles and
new edges to perceive it.

There is a need to strip back and
focus on what you have.

The light of Lemuria is one of
diamond purity and simplicity,

Working in alignment with the heart to live
in peace and harmony with the Earth."

Lemurian Crystal

Talking to the limestone giants
at Avebury stone circle.

About the Author

Katie-Jane Wright is a spiritual author, crystal whisperer and guardian, ceremonialist, healer and teacher based in the UK. Her healing lineage was active from a young age, when she began seeing and working with spirits of many dimensions, her healing hands passed down through her mother line. She is keen to help others remember the ways we used to work with the stones in the past, and the multi-dimensional ways we can work with them now. She offers transformational crystal workshops, events and healing retreats around the world, with a focus on crystals and sound.

She created her brand &Crystals in 2016, aiming to teach people how to connect with energies through their heart. Through her store she sells small collections of rare minerals and crystals skulls, all handpicked and sourced from collectors who are guided to her. The integrity of the stones and connection with the land and people they came from is of the utmost importance to her. She works with small family mines in Brazil in an ethical and sustainable way.

This wish for respect and integrity can be found woven through the oracle deck that is a companion to this crystal book: *The Song of the Stones Oracle*, where she has journeyed with the land and guardians of the stones to tell their stories. Her healing crystals collections have been sold in Anthropology stores worldwide. Katie-Jane has written another crystal book called *Crystals: A Conscious Guide*, as well as oracle decks *Spirit Animal Wisdom* and *Earth Alchemy*, with illustrations by Nikki Strange.

Work With Me

I have a series of high-frequency crystal courses, including "New Earth Crystal Frequencies", "The Magdalene Crystal Codes" and "Diamond Sun Lightbody Activations", as well as a library of 90-minute downloadable crystal workshops. These are available on my website: katiejanewright.com and through andcrystals.com

I hold retreats, women's circles, grid activations and events in Glastonbury, Mexico, the USA and France, and I am always open to collaborations as well as crystalline sound, breath work and wrapping workshops in my yurt in the UK. Keep up to date with my offerings through my newsletter at andcrystals.com

Purchase Stones

If you would like to purchase crystals or sound instruments from me you can find me atandcrystals.com. I handpick small, curated collections of rare and hard-to-find crystals with emphasis on Lemurian stones, crystal skulls and dragon carvings. They are always held, cared for and truly alive, so they reach you in the most awake and attuned state.

Acknowledgements

I want to thank Caitlin Callahan for her amazing photography for this book, for adventuring with me, for loving me, and always capturing the beauty of the Earth. It was truly uplifting to have your support through this journey.

Thank you to my Watkins family for saying "yes" to this book, and supporting me along the way. Sophie and Cat, thank you. And lastly it goes without saying that I am grateful to my ancestors for paving the way, for the love and stories, the heart and soul of this book. It could not have been written without the ancestors of many lineages pouring their love for the Earth into it. I hope the love shines through.

We are truly blessed to be living on this planet at this time: I love the Earth so dearly. Thank you for journeying with me.

The *Song of the Stones Oracle Deck*,
a companion deck to this book.